CHILDREN'S
ENCYCLOPEDIA
OF UNEXPLAINED
MYSTERIES

ARCTURUS

Picture Credits:

Every attempt has been made to clear copyright. Should there be any inadvertent omission, please apply to the publisher for rectification.
Interiors: AKG: 11; Bill Stoneham: 90; Corbis: 9, 24, 28, 65, 77, 85; Frank Joseph: 80; Idaho State University: 105; Mary Evans Picture Library: 15, 19, 31, 33, 62, 68, 112; P. Gray: 58; Paul Oakley: 1; R Jacobs: 110; Science Photo Library: 5; Shutterstock: 12, 17, 20, 21, 23, 26, 36, 38, 41, 44, 46, 49, 51, 57, 61, 66, 71, 72, 75, 78, 82, 87, 88, 92, 94, 97, 98, 101, 116; T. Boyer: 53, 55; TopFoto: 6, 34, 43, 109; Wikimedia: 107. Wikipedia.com: 115; William Stoneham: 102, 119, 121, 123.
Front cover: Main image: Paul Oakley. All other images Shutterstock. Back cover: Shutterstock

ARCTURUS

First published in 2013. This edition published in 2021 by Arcturus Publishing Limited
26/27 Bickels Yard, 151–153 Bermondsey Street,
London SE1 3HA

Author: Stuart Webb
Editors: Lisa Regan and Susie Rae
Designers: Jane Hawkins and Trudi Webb
Managing Editor: Joe Harris
Design Manager: Jessica Holliland

ISBN: 978-1-3988-0943-7
CH008653US
Supplier 29, Date 0621, Print run 11342

Printed in China

Contents

Chapter 1

Ghosts

Throughout history and all over the world, people have told each other stories of encounters with ghosts and spirits. Is this widespread experience evidence of the survival of the soul after death? Or does it tell us more about the way that we can be deceived by our senses? This chapter brings together a collection of extraordinary, seemingly inexplicable tales of hauntings from different times and places. However, no one can prove beyond doubt the accuracy of these accounts. And it is worth remembering that ghost stories, like any other stories, can become embellished in the retelling.

Ancient Spirits

There is evidence that ancient peoples all over the world had a strong belief in the afterlife. Prehistoric cave paintings suggest that early humans attempted to communicate with their dead ancestors. The ancient Egyptians believed that when someone died, their soul left their body. The soul would then return and be reunited with the body after it was buried.

Greek Ghost

One early account of a spectral encounter was recorded by the Greek philosopher Athenodorus, who lived during the 1st century BCE. Against the advice of his friends, Athenodorus agreed to rent a room in a lodging house that was reputed to be haunted. At nightfall his nerves were apparently tested by the appearance of a gaunt-faced spirit of an old man draped in the soiled robes of the grave. The ghost, so the story goes, was weighed down by chains and appeared to be in anguish, but was unable to communicate what it was that bound him to that place.

The ghost led Athenodorus along a narrow passage

and out into the garden, whereupon it faded into the bushes. Athenodorus noted where the spirit had disappeared and the next morning he informed the magistrates who ordered workmen to excavate the garden. There they unearthed a skeleton weighed down by rusted chains. The corpse appeared to be that of a murder victim. They then had the skeleton reburied according to Greek funeral rites.

Am I Beautiful?

One of the most frightening of ancient ghost stories comes from the Heian period (794–1185 CE) in Japan. Kuchisake-onna is a spiteful spirit in Japanese folklore.

According to the legend, the Kuchisake-onna wanders through the fog, her face covered with a mask, seeking solitary young men and women. She asks them: "Watashi kirei?" (Am I beautiful?). If they answer "yes," she tears off the mask revealing that the corners of her mouth stretch from ear to ear. She repeats her question and if they keep their nerve and again answer "yes," she allows them to go on their way. But if they run screaming, she pursues them shrieking with fury. Methods of escaping the wrath of the Kuchisake-onna include telling her she is of average beauty or distracting her with money. The story is so deeply rooted in Japanese culture that as recently as 1979 there was public panic when stories spread that the Kuchisake-onna had been seen.

Many people throughout history have believed that we have not just a physical body, but a separate spiritual body, which can live after death.

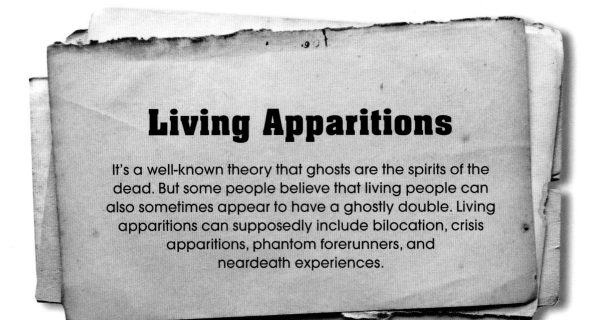

Living Apparitions

It's a well-known theory that ghosts are the spirits of the dead. But some people believe that living people can also sometimes appear to have a ghostly double. Living apparitions can supposedly include bilocation, crisis apparitions, phantom forerunners, and neardeath experiences.

Bilocation

There are some documented cases where living people have apparently projected a double of themselves to another place. The most famous example is that of the French school teacher Emilie Sagee. Miss Sagee was a popular addition to the staff at the Neuwelcke Finishing School for Young Ladies in Livonia (a region in present-day Latvia and Estonia) in 1845, but there was something unsettling about her that her pupils could not put into words. She was pretty, capable, and conscientious but at the same time distracted, as if her mind was elsewhere. The trouble was that it was not only her mind that was elsewhere. Supposedly, so was her doppelgänger, her spirit double.

For weeks there had been stories that Miss Sagee had been seen in two parts of the school at the same time. Naturally, her colleagues scoffed at the very idea and dismissed it as schoolgirl gossip, but they soon began to think that there was more to Emilie than met the eye. One of her pupils, Antoine von Wrangel, was unusually

According to paranormal investigators, it is possible for living people to appear in one location while they are in reality elsewhere.

anxious the day she prepared for a high society party. Even so, her girlish excitement cannot account for what she thought she saw when she looked over her shoulder to admire herself in the mirror. There, attending to the hem of her dress, appeared to be not one but two Mademoiselle Sagees. Not surprisingly, the poor girl fainted on the spot. Not long afterward, a class of 13 girls allegedly saw Miss Sagee's doppelgänger standing next to its more solid counterpart at the blackboard one day, mimicking the movements of the "real" Emilie.

Eventually, these stories reached the ears of the headmistress, but there were no grounds for a reprimand, never mind a dismissal. Emilie continued to be a conscientious member of the staff. The next summer, matters came to a head.

The entire school was assembled one morning in a room overlooking the garden where Miss Sagee could be seen picking flowers. But when the supervising teacher left the room, another Miss Sagee reportedly appeared in her chair as if from nowhere. Outside, the "real" Emilie could still be clearly seen gathering flowers, although her movements appeared to be sluggish, as if her vitality had drained away. So the story goes, two of the more inquisitive girls took the opportunity to step forward and gingerly touch the double in the chair. To one it felt like cloth, but not entirely solid. Another girl purportedly passed right through the apparition by walking between the table and the chair. The doppelgänger apparently remained still and lifeless. Moments later it allegedly faded and the girls observed that the real Emilie became

TALE OF THE PARANORMAL
THE ABSENT MP

In 1905, British MP Sir Frederick Carne Rasch apparently appeared in the House of Commons at the same moment that his body lay in bed suffering from influenza. Sir Frederick had been so anxious to attend the debate that he had supposedly willed himself to appear, but his concentration must have weakened because he allegedly vanished before the vote was taken. When he returned to Parliament a few days later, MPs delighted in prodding him to see if he was really there in the flesh.

herself again, moving among the flower beds with some purpose.

The girls quizzed Miss Sagee, but all she could remember was that when she had seen the teacher leave the room she wished that she could have been there to supervise the class until their teacher returned. It seems that her thoughts had preceded her.

Ghost Files

CRISIS APPARITIONS

Sometimes, it is said that the figure of a living person can be seen when that person is in danger or close to death. This is known as a crisis apparition. Crisis apparitions may appear to loved ones or strangers, who may be far away at the time. They can also manifest as a voice with some message or warning. The person in crisis is said to be unaware that they are doing this.

Cry for Help

One of the earliest recorded examples of a crisis apparition occurred in 1828. In that year, Robert Bruce was the first mate aboard a cargo ship cutting through the icy waters off the Canadian coast. During the voyage he entered the captain's cabin where he claimed to find a stranger bent over a slate, writing intensely and in great haste. The figure, he said, appeared solid, but there was an other-worldly aspect to him and a grave expression on his face that unnerved Bruce. When the stranger raised his head and looked at him, Bruce fled, fearing that the presence of the phantom foretold disaster for all on board. He found the skipper on deck and persuaded him to return to the cabin. "I never was a believer in ghosts," said Bruce as they made their way below deck, "but if the truth must be told sir, I'd rather not face it alone." But when they entered the cabin it was empty. However,

they apparently found the slate and on it were scrawled the words "Steer to the nor'west."

At first the skipper suspected that the crew was playing a practical joke, so he ordered them all to copy the message. After comparing their handwriting with the original he had to admit he could not identify the culprit. A search of the entire ship failed to find any stowaways, leaving the captain with an unusual dilemma: to ignore the message and risk having the lives of untold lost souls on his conscience, or change his course and risk being thought of as a superstitious old fool in the eyes of the crew. He chose to change course.

Just in Time

Fortunately, he had made the right decision. Within hours they came upon a stricken vessel that had been critically damaged by an iceberg. There were only minutes to save the passengers and crew before it sank beneath the waves. Bruce watched with grim satisfaction and relief as the survivors were brought aboard, but then he claimed to see something that haunted him to his dying day. He said he came face to face with the stranger he had seen scrawling the message earlier that day in the captain's cabin.

After the man had recovered sufficiently to be questioned, Bruce and the captain asked him to copy the message on the slate. They compared the two sets of handwriting. There was no question about it—they were identical. Initially, the stranger couldn't account for his presence on the ship, until he recalled a dream that he had had about the same time that Bruce had seen his "ghost" in the captain's cabin. After falling asleep from exhaustion he had dreamed that he was aboard a ship that was coming to rescue him and his fellow survivors. He told the others of his dream to reassure them that help was on its way and he even described the rescue ship, all of which reportedly proved correct in every detail. The captain of the wrecked ship confirmed his story. "He described her appearance and rig," he told their rescuers, "and to our utter astonishment, when your vessel hove in sight, she corresponded exactly to his description of her."

After following a "ghostly" message, the crew of Robert Bruce's cargo ship came upon a stricken vessel.

Near-Death Experiences

Near-death experiences have been reported by people who have been, at some stage, physically and medically dead—that is to say, they show no vital signs of life. Although no two reports of near-death experiences are the same, they do tend to share some common qualities. Many people claim that they feel as if they have risen out of their body. Often they look down upon the medical teams trying to bring them back to life. Indeed, many people who have had near-death experiences can state exactly what happened, who said what, and which instruments were used to resuscitate them. Other experiences involve the person reportedly hovering above members of their family at the time of death.

Sometimes they say that seeing their close relations was enough to force them to return to their bodies. If not, they often report that a feeling of sublime peace and joy sweeps over them. They say they find themselves in a dark tunnel with a beautiful white or golden light at the end of it. Sometimes they claim to hear the voices of deceased loved ones, or even God, telling them to return to Earth. They may then return to their bodies voluntarily or be revived through medical means.

In 2001, *The Lancet* medical journal published a report of a thirteen-year study into near-death experiences that occurred in Dutch hospitals. The investigation was conducted by cardiologist Pim van Lommel and involved the questioning of 344 patients immediately after they had been resuscitated. Twelve percent had a "deep" experience—that is, an experience of leaving the body, seeing a bright light, or meeting dead relatives. Interestingly, the details of their experiences remained the same, even when they were reinterviewed two and eight years later. It was also noted that those who had near-death experiences became noticeably more appreciative of life, and had much less fear of death.

EYEWITNESS ACCOUNT

LIKE A SOAP BUBBLE

Dr. A.S. Wiltse of Kansas described his own near-death experience, after contracting typhoid fever and lapsing into unconsciousness in 1889:

"I learned that the epidermis (skin) was the outside boundary of the ultimate tissues, so to speak, of the soul.... As I emerged from the head I floated up and down ... like a soap bubble ... until I at last broke loose from the body and fell lightly to the floor, where I slowly rose and expanded into the full stature of a man."

Phantom Forerunners

A phantom forerunner occurs when a person is apparently preceded to a place by his or her spirit double, like a physical prophecy. Some phantom forerunners are said to warn of death. Others apparently take the form of phone calls rather than physical appearances.

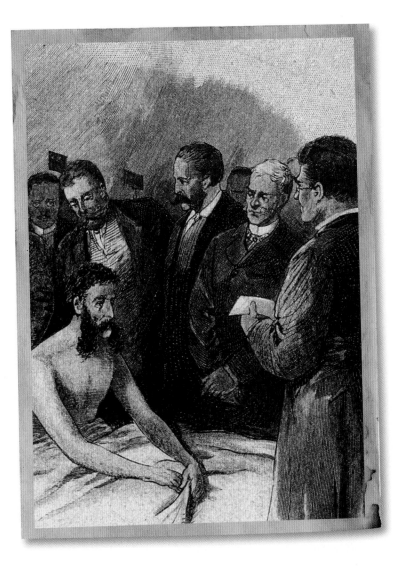

TALE OF THE PARANORMAL

GETTING AHEAD OF THEMSELVES

The Reverend W. Mountford of Boston was visiting a friend when he looked out of the dining room window and apparently saw a carriage approaching the rear of the house. "Your guests have arrived," said Mountford, whereupon his host joined him at the window. Both men claimed they observed the carriage turn the corner as if it were going to the entrance. But no one rang the door bell and the servants did not announce the arrival of their visitors. Instead, the host's niece entered looking rather flustered having walked all the way from her home, and informed Mountford and his host that her parents had just passed her without acknowledging her or offering her a lift. Ten minutes later the real carriage arrived with the host's brother and his wife. They denied all knowledge of having passed their daughter en route.

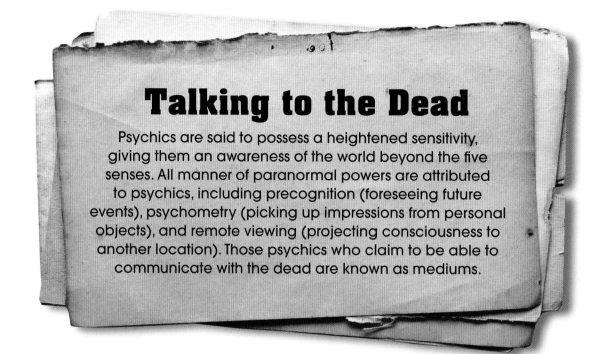

Talking to the Dead

Psychics are said to possess a heightened sensitivity, giving them an awareness of the world beyond the five senses. All manner of paranormal powers are attributed to psychics, including precognition (foreseeing future events), psychometry (picking up impressions from personal objects), and remote viewing (projecting consciousness to another location). Those psychics who claim to be able to communicate with the dead are known as mediums.

Message from the Mother-in-Law

Karin Page, from Kent, England, claimed to have been seeing ghosts since the age of six, but, she says, it took a message from the "other side" to finally convince her of the survival of the soul. "One day my elderly mother-in-law promised me that she would come back after her death. I didn't take it seriously, but two months after her passing, all the clocks in the house started behaving strangely. They all showed a different time

Many witnesses to "ghostly" activity allege that clocks and watches are strangely affected by the passage of spirits through the material world.

COLD READING

Mediums are often accused of using a technique called "cold reading." This involves making informed guesses about an individual based on their body language, the way they speak, and other clues such as their appearance and background. A skilled cold reader can use this kind of guesswork, combined with an understanding of probability, to make it appear that they are reading someone's mind or are being given messages by a spirit. It is absolutely beyond doubt that some so-called "mediums" use these techniques. But this doesn't necessarily rule out the possibility that some practitioners have genuine supernatural powers.

and an alarm clock rolled off the shelf just as I was telling my daughter about how oddly they were all behaving. Another day, the phone jumped off its holder on the wall and started swinging from side to side. Then the electric blanket and toaster switched themselves on. Each time I felt a chill in the air. It was Mary trying to tell me that she was with me.

"The final proof came when I went to a spiritualist meeting and was told by a medium, who I'd never met before, that my husband's mother was trying to communicate, that her name was Mary, and that she had died of cancer, both of which were true. She just wanted to say thank you for all the time I had looked after her. Then the medium said that Mary sent her love to my husband, my son, and his girlfriend and she named them all, which left me speechless. The only thing I couldn't understand was when she said, "I'm with Emma now," because I didn't know of an Emma in the family. Afterward, I found out Emma had been Mary's sister who had died eleven years earlier. Since then I have smelled Mary's talcum powder on many occasions and I know then that she is watching over me."

Final Message

English medium Jill Nash sees a medium's role as helping the bereaved attain closure by facilitating a reunion with their loved ones. "On one particularly memorable occasion I opened the door expecting to see a little elderly lady and instead saw her and her late husband. He walked in behind her. She was, of course, unaware that he was with her but I could see him plain as day, although he was fainter than a living person, almost transparent, and there was nothing to see below the knee. He was tall and slim and when she sat down he stood behind her with a satisfied grin on his face as if he was thinking, 'At last, now I can tell her what I have been trying to say to her for months.' He asked me to tell her that he often stood behind her, and that if she felt something brushing against her cheek or a gentle pat on the head that it was only him reassuring her that he was still around. And as soon as I said that, she admitted that she had felt these things and had wondered if it was him."

Possession

Possession is said to occur when a spirit, demon, or some other discarnate entity takes control of a human body, causing changes in health and actions. The idea of dead souls or other forces taking over the bodies of the living sounds scary, but, according to some, it can be for a benign purpose, as in the case of Lurancy Vennum.

The Vennum Case

In the summer of 1877, Mary Lurancy Vennum, a 13-year-old girl from Watseka, Illinois, suffered a series of convulsions, falling into a trancelike state for hours at a time. All efforts to awaken her failed. While she was in this state she spoke of seeing angels and a brother and sister who had died some years earlier. Shortly after this, Lurancy was apparently subdued by a succession of dominant personalities who spoke through her, including a crotchety old woman called Katrina Hogan. The family resigned themselves to having their daughter committed to an asylum, but then a family named Roff intervened.

The Roffs persuaded Lurancy's parents to consult a doctor from Wisconsin who had treated their own daughter, also with the name of Mary, in the months before she died. Mary Roff had suffered similar "fits" in which she demonstrated supposedly clairvoyant abilities such as being able to read through a blindfold.

When Dr. Stevens visited the Vennum house on February 1, 1878, Katrina Hogan was supposedly in control. At first she was cold and aloof, gazing into space and ordering Dr. Stevens to leave her be whenever he attempted to come near. But his persistence paid off and before long, Dr. Stevens was able to draw out "Katrina's" personal history. Soon another personality seemed to appear: a young man named Willie Canning whose hold on Lurancy was erratic and offered little of value that the doctor could verify. With the parents' permission Dr. Stevens tried hypnosis and Lurancy reasserted herself but remained in a trance. She spoke of having been possessed of evil spirits, but that may have been her interpretation conditioned by her strict religious upbringing. Then events took an even more interesting turn.

Becoming Mary

Lurancy announced that she could see other spirits around her, one of whom was Mary Roff. Lurancy did not know Mary Roff, who had died when Lurancy was just a year old, nor had she visited the Roff home up to that point. Mrs. Roff was present when her "Mary" came through, speaking through Lurancy, but there is no suggestion that Lurancy was faking to impress or ingratiate herself with the dead girl's mother. The next morning "Mary" calmly announced her intention to go "home," by which she meant the Roff household.

On February 11, the Vennums agreed to let their daughter go. On the way there, they passed the Roff's old house where their daughter had died and "Mary" insisted on being taken there, but she was eventually persuaded that it was no longer the family home. When she arrived at the new house she appeared to know the relatives who greeted her.

Was Lurancy Genuine?

The Lurancy case was reviewed by psychologist Frank Hoffmann. He said that the grieving Roff family encouraged Lurancy to believe that she was Mary. Another investigator, Henry Bruce, pointed out that the "Mary personality" only appeared when the Roffs were present and disappeared entirely when Mary Lurancy got married.

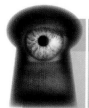

EYEWITNESS ACCOUNT

FAMILIAR TUNES

When Lurancy Vennum was first brought into the Roff home, she saw a piano that Mary used to play. She approached it and said, "Oh, Ma! The same old piano—and the same old cover!" She opened the case of the instrument and attempted to play and sing. The songs were those of Mary Roff's youth, prompting a member of the Roff family to say: "As we stood listening, the familiar ones were hers, although emanating from another's lips."

Was the Lurancy Vennum case wishful thinking on the part of the Roff family? Or were there supernatural forces at work?

15

Reincarnated Sisters?

John Pollock had lost his first two daughters, Joanna, 11, and Jacqueline, 6, in May 1957, in a car accident near their home in Hexham, Northumberland. Pollock, a devout Roman Catholic, assumed that God had taken his girls to punish him for believing in reincarnation. However, a year later, when his wife learned that she was pregnant, Pollock became convinced that the souls of the two girls would be reborn in order to demonstrate that the Church was wrong to deny the natural process of death and rebirth. When his wife's doctor informed the couple that they were to expect a single child, Pollock assured him he was wrong—there would be twins, both girls. On October 4, 1958, he was proved correct.

The twins were monozygotic (meaning they developed from a single egg), yet the second twin, Jennifer, was born with a thin white line on her forehead in the same place that her dead sister Jacqueline had sustained a wound while falling from her bicycle. Her parents were also puzzled by the appearance of a distinctive birth mark on her left hip, identical to the one that Jacqueline had.

Ghost Files

REINCARNATION

Reincarnation is a belief in which the soul or spirit comes back to life in a new form, following the death of the body. Most Indian religious traditions believe in reincarnation, and in recent decades people in the West have developed an interest in the idea. There have been several scientific studies into the phenomenon. Over a period of 40 years, psychiatrist Ian Stevenson investigated 2,500 reports of young children who claimed to remember a past life. He compared children's statements with the known facts of the life of the deceased person they identified with, and he matched birthmarks and birth defects to wounds and scars on the deceased. Stevenson believed that his strict methods ruled out all possible "normal" explanations for the children's memories.

Strange Knowledge

The girls grew up in Whitley Bay, but when they were three and a half their father took them back to Hexham. He claimed that the girls pointed out places they had never seen and talked about where they had played. He said they knew when they were approaching their school, although it was out of sight, and they apparently identified their old home as they passed it, although their father had said nothing.

Six months later, they were given Joanna and Jacqueline's toy box. They allegedly called all their dead sisters' dolls by name. Their mother, Florence, also claimed she observed them playing a game she found disturbing. Jennifer lay on the floor with her head in Gillian's lap, play-acting that she was dying and her sister would say, "The blood's coming out of your eyes. That's where the car hit you." Neither parent had discussed the accident with the children.

On another occasion their mother said she heard them screaming in the street. When she came out, she saw them clutching each other and looking terrified in the direction of a stationary car with its motor running. The girls were crying, "The car! It's coming at us!"

The possibility that they might be the reincarnation of their elder, deceased sisters brought no comfort to their mother, who could not reconcile this with the Church's edict that belief in reincarnation was a mortal sin. To Florence Pollock's relief, however, the incident with the car marked the end of the affair. At the age of five, the girls abruptly ceased to exhibit these strange actions, and developed into normal, healthy children.

According to Buddhist tradition, living creatures are reborn again and again in a cycle known as samsara.

Haunted Houses

Ghosts are often associated with particular houses or buildings. Traditionally, such ghosts were the victims of violent or tragic events in the building's past, such as murder, accidental death, or suicide. So-called haunted houses are usually old, but many aren't. Ghosts have been sighted in the homes of celebrities, prisons, and even a Toys 'R' Us store.

The Bloody Tower

If any site deserves its formidable reputation for spectral sightings it is the Tower of London, whose weathered stones are soaked in the blood of countless executed martyrs and traitors. It is said that the walls still echo with the screams of those who were tortured there during the most violent chapters in English history.

Among the Tower's most illustrious residents were the young princes Edward and Richard who were imprisoned in the so-called Bloody Tower by their ambitious uncle, the Duke of Gloucester, in 1483. It is believed by some that the duke ordered their murder so that he could be crowned King Richard III. The princes have been sighted several times walking hand in hand through the chilly corridors after dusk, possibly in search of their murderous uncle.

TALE OF THE PARANORMAL

THE NINE DAYS QUEEN

Arguably the most tragic figure to haunt the Tower of London is Lady Jane Grey, who was a pawn in the Duke of Northumberland's plot to usurp the English crown from the rightful heir, Mary Tudor. Lady Jane, who was only 15, ruled for just nine days before she was arrested and condemned to death in February 1554. Her grieving ghost has apparently been sighted by several witnesses. In 1957, two sentries swore they witnessed the apparition of the young queen form from a ball of light on the roof of the Salt Tower.

Anne Boleyn, the second wife of Henry VIII, is said to still walk in the Tower Chapel where she made her peace with God before she was beheaded in 1536. She is reported to have been seen leading a spectral procession through the chapel both with and without her head.

Another headless ghost—that of James Crofts Scott, the illegitimate son of King Charles II—is said to walk the battlements connecting the Bell and Beauchamp Towers dressed in cavalier attire. Apparently, James was not satisfied with being made Duke of Monmouth as compensation for losing the crown to his uncle, James II, in 1685, and chose to assert his claim by force of arms. His rebellion was short-lived and he paid for his disloyalty by forfeiting his head.

Singular Execution of the Countess of Salisbury in 1541.

The Executioner's Pursuit

One of the most famous episodes in the Tower's history was the botched execution of Margaret Pole, Countess of Salisbury. Margaret was 70 years old when she was condemned to death in 1541 by Henry VIII, even though she posed no threat to his dynasty. Standing resolutely on the scaffold, the story goes, she refused to submit to the hooded executioner, who waited for her to rest her head on the block, but instead she commanded him to sever her head from her neck where she stood. When he refused, she fled, forcing him to pursue her around Tower Green swinging his weapon.

It is said that if you are brave enough to remain in the Tower after dark on May 27, the anniversary of her execution, you can

Lady Margaret Pole was found guilty of treason, but refused to kneel for the executioner, instead fleeing for her life.

see the scene reenacted by the principal players themselves as Margaret's ghost tries once again to outrun her executioner.

Lincoln's Ghost

President Abraham Lincoln was a firm believer in the afterlife and enthusiastically participated in séances during his tenure in office prior to his assassination in 1865. He confided in his wife that he had a premonition of his own death. He dreamed that he was walking through the White House when he heard the sound of weeping coming from the East Room. When he entered he saw an open coffin surrounded by mourners and guarded by a detachment of Union soldiers. He asked one of the guards who it was who lay in the coffin, to be told, "The President. He was killed by an assassin." Lincoln then approached the coffin and saw his own corpse.

Since his death, many people claim to have seen Lincoln's ghost stalking the White House. The wife of President Calvin Coolidge entertained guests to the White House with her recollections of the day she entered the Oval Office and saw Lincoln looking out across the Potomac with his hands clasped behind his back—a habit he acquired during the Civil War.

It is known that Eleanor Roosevelt held séances in the White House during World War II, and she claimed to be in contact with the spirit of Lincoln. Queen Wilhelmina of the Netherlands, who was a guest of the Roosevelts during their time at the White

LINCOLN

President Lincoln's ghost, many believe, has haunted the White House ever since his death.

House, reported being awoken in the night by a knock on her bedroom door. Thinking that it might be Eleanor Roosevelt, she got out of bed, put on her nightgown, and opened the door. There, so she claimed, stood the ghost of Abe Lincoln.

President Harry Truman often complained that he was prevented from working by Lincoln's ghost who would repeatedly knock on his door when he was attempting to draft an important speech.

TALE OF THE PARANORMAL

A REVEALING ENCOUNTER

Winston Churchill was a frequent visitor to the White House during World War II and he often indulged in a hot bath, together with a cigar and a glass of whisky. One evening, so he claimed, he climbed out of the bath and went into the adjoining bedroom to look for a towel when he noticed a man standing by the fireplace. It was Abraham Lincoln. Unperturbed, Churchill said sorry for his state of undress: "Good evening, Mr. President. You seem to have me at a disadvantage." Lincoln is said to have smiled and tactfully withdrawn.

Alcatraz

Long before Alcatraz Island in San Francisco Bay was converted into a prison to house America's most notorious criminals, Native Americans warned the US army not to build a fortress on "the Rock" as it was the dwelling place of evil spirits. Needless to say, their warnings were ignored. When the fortress was converted into a military prison in 1912, several inmates were said to have become mentally disturbed by mysterious noises in the night, by cold spots that turned their breath to mist, even on warm summer evenings, and by the sight of two burning red eyes, which they claimed to have seen in the cells on the lower level.

TALE OF THE PARANORMAL

THE HOLE

Even the most hardened inmates at Alcatraz feared being thrown into "the hole," the windowless cells of D Block, where a red-eyed demon was said to be waiting to consume lost souls. On one memorable night during the 1940s, a prisoner was hurled screaming into solitary in 14D and continued yelling until early the next morning. When the guards finally opened his cell, they found him dead. An autopsy was conducted and the official cause of death was determined to be "non-self-inflicted strangulation."

The story gets more extraordinary when, according to the sworn statement of an eyewitness, the prisoners were lined up for roll-call the next morning and the number didn't tally. There was one extra prisoner in the line. So a guard walked along the line looking at each face to see if one of the inmates was playing a trick on him. He came face to face with the dead man who had died in the night and who promptly vanished before his eyes. The guard later related this story to others and swore on the life of his children that it was true.

Scaring the Tourists

Since the Rock opened to tourists, visitors have claimed to have seen cell doors closing by themselves and to have heard the sound of sobbing, moaning, and phantom footsteps, the screams of prisoners, as well as the delirious cries of those made ill or traumatized by their confinement. Others have spoken of seeing phantom soldiers and prisoners pass along the corridors and out through solid walls, and many have complained of being watched even though the corridors and cells were empty.

Some of those brave enough to try out one of the bunks for size have claimed to have found themselves pinned down by a weight on their chest as the previous occupant made his presence known and showed his resentment at having his privacy invaded. In the lower cells, 12 and 14 in particular, tourists have reported picking up feelings of despair, panic, and pain, and they have excused themselves to catch a breath of fresh air. When a thermometer has been placed in cell 14D (see column, left), it has apparently measured the air temperature as many degrees colder than the other cells in that block.

And what of the Rock's most notorious inmate, Al "Scarface" Capone? Well, Capone may have been a dangerous gangster on the outside but in the "big house" he was apparently a model prisoner who sat quietly on his bunk in cell B206 learning to play the banjo. It is said that if you sit quietly in that cell you can hear the

According to Native American tradition, the Rock was the dwelling place of evil spirits, and anyone living there was in peril.

ghostly strains of Capone whiling away eternity playing popular tunes of the Roaring '20s.

Edgar Allen Poe's House

The spirit of Edgar Allen Poe, author of numerous tales of terror, haunts both American literature and also—allegedly—the house in Baltimore where he lived as a young man in the 1830s. The narrow brick house at 203 North Amity Street is said to be so spooky that even local gangs are scared to break in. When the police arrived to investigate a reported burglary in 1968, they reported seeing a light in the ground floor window floating up to reappear on the second floor and then in the attic, but when they entered the property, there was no one to be seen.

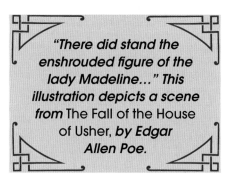
it is claimed, doors and windows have opened and closed by themselves, visitors have been tapped on the shoulder, and disembodied voices have been heard. Psychic investigators have also reported seeing a stout, silvery haired old woman dressed in clothing of the period gliding through the rooms.

In a twist of which Poe himself might have been perversely proud, local parents still use the ghost of the horror writer to terrify their children into doing what they are told. Poe has become the bogeyman of Baltimore.

Toys 'R' Us

The Toys 'R' Us superstore in Sunnyvale, California, occupied a substantial plot on what had been a ranch and an apple orchard back in the 19th century. Some believe that the poltergeist activity witnessed there was connected with the previous owner, John Murphy, who, it appears, disliked children, not to mention the commercial development of his former home.

Each morning, employees apparently arrived to find stock scattered across the floor and items placed on the wrong

Even in daylight the house is unsettling. An eerie portrait of Poe's wife, painted as she lay in her coffin, hangs in one room, her melancholic gaze following visitors around the room. Local residents have also reported seeing a shadowy figure working at a desk at a second floor-window, although Poe worked in the attic.

The curator has apparently recorded many incidents of poltergeist activity and this seems to originate in the bedroom that belonged to Poe's grandmother. Here, shelves. Turnover in staff increased when sensitive staff members claimed they heard a voice calling their name and were then touched by invisible hands. The fragrant scent of fresh flowers unsettled several employees. All these reports brought the matter to the attention of the local press and ghost buffs around the globe in 1978.

As a result, local journalist Antoinette May and psychic Sylvia Brown camped out in the store overnight with a photographer and a number of "ghost catchers." Once the staff had left for the night and the lights were dimmed, Sylvia said she began to sense a male presence approaching the group. In her mind's eye she "saw" a tall, thin man striding down the aisle toward her. In her head she heard him speak with a Swedish accent, identifying himself as Johnny Johnson.

Sylvia claimed that he told her his story. She said that he had come to California

in the mid-1800s from Pennsylvania where he had succumbed to an inflammation of the brain, which affected his conduct. This appears to account for his nickname "Crazy Johnny." He had worked on the Murphy family farm where he formed an unrequited passion for Murphy's daughter Elizabeth. According to news reports from the time, Johnny suffered a wound while chopping wood in the orchard and had bled to death.

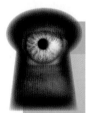

The Town Too Tough to Die

They called Tombstone, Arizona, "the town too tough to die," and it appears that certain of its most notorious inhabitants are equally reluctant to go quietly. The town is now preserved as a national museum with many of the old buildings lovingly restored to their former rickety glory and stocked with original artifacts from its violent past, including the hearse that transported bodies to Boot Hill, the hangman's noose, and the honky-tonk piano, which accompanied many a barroom brawl. Some say that if you stay after closing time you can hear the piano playing "Red River Valley," a popular cowboy tune, and hear the echo of their raucous laughter.

This photo of Tombstone dates from 1885. The town suffered two major fires in 1881 and 1882. By the mid-1880s, the place was virtually abandoned.

Saloon Spirits

The tour guides are fond of telling visitors that as many as 31 ghosts are thought to haunt the Bird Cage Theater saloon, which was the site of 26 killings—a fact borne out by the 140 bullet holes that can be seen peppering the ceiling. The phantom most frequently seen in the saloon is a stage hand dressed in black striped trousers, wearing a card dealer's visor, and carrying a clipboard. He is said to appear from nowhere, walk across the stage and exit through the facing wall.

Tourists have also reported seeing the ghost of a young boy who died of yellow fever in 1882, and hearing an unidentified woman sighing plaintively as if pining for her lost love. Others have commented on how impressed they have been by the authenticity of the actors' clothes in the gambling room and the dancehall, only to be told that the museum doesn't employ actors, and nor does it ask its staff to dress in period costumes. One female member of staff, who works in the gift shop on the ground floor of the Bird Cage Theater, swears she once saw on a security monitor a lady in a white dress walking through the cellar at closing time when all the visitors had left.

Since it is a museum, no one is allowed to smoke inside the buildings. Nevertheless, visitors often remark on the strong smell of cigar smoke that lingers round the card tables, and some have spoken of the delicate scent of lilac perfume in the backstage bathroom. Equally odd is the $100 poker chip that allegedly appeared on the poker table one day, then promptly vanished after being locked away in a desk, before turning up in a filing cabinet some days later.

There have been other mysterious goings-on. Staff claim that furniture has moved by itself, and a tour guide was apparently struck on the back of the knee, causing him to fall to the floor. When he looked round, he said there was no one in sight. The old saloon also contains a notorious "cold spot," where the temperature is said to be noticeably chillier than the warm air surrounding it.

Ghost Files

HISTORY OF TOMBSTONE

The streets of Tombstone were the setting for numerous showdowns, the most famous being the gunfight at the OK Corral when Marshall Wyatt Earp, his brothers, and their consumptive, trigger-happy friend Doc Holliday faced down the Clanton and McLaury gang, three of whom were killed. In the aftermath, the surviving Clantons and their friends took their bloody revenge. Virgil Earp was shot in the back while playing pool in the Bird Cage Theater, the town's notorious saloon, and his dying words are said to echo there after dark.

Chapter 2

UFOs

The modern UFO phenomenon began with the alleged sighting of "flying saucers", or unidentified flying objects (UFOs), by American pilot Kenneth Arnold in 1947. Many books on the subject describe Arnold's encounter as the first UFO sighting, although it was not acknowledged as such at the time.

Many UFOlogists believe that Earth has regularly been visited by aliens since the 1940s.

Flying Saucers

Back in 1947, neither Arnold nor anyone else was even thinking about aliens or UFOs. It was assumed that what he had seen was some kind of top-secret military aircraft of revolutionary design. Nor was Arnold's the first sighting of such objects. It was merely the first to make it into the national and international press. For that we must thank the reporter who took Arnold's description of the mysterious aircraft he had seen and dubbed them "flying saucers." The name caught the public imagination and made good newspaper copy.

The story took a dramatic new twist when it became clear that what Arnold believed he had seen did not accord with any secret weapon belonging to the United States. The speed, design, and motion of the aircraft Arnold described were utterly unlike anything being developed at the time. The first thought to spring to the minds of most people in aviation was that the USA's Cold War rival, the Soviet Union, had developed some startling new technology. However, Arnold's aircraft seemed so far in advance of anything the Russians had used during World War II, which had ended only two years earlier, that this seemed rather unlikely.

Sightings Multiply

It was not long before people all across the USA started coming forward with their own sightings of mysterious aircraft. It may be that these people had been reluctant to speak publicly before – either because they feared ridicule or because they were unaware that they had seen anything particularly odd. Like Arnold, they may have assumed that they were seeing some secret new type of aircraft. After all, at this time jets, rockets, and helicopters were all new inventions that remained shrouded in mystery. There seemed to be no limit to the inventiveness of aircraft engineers.

At this early stage the reports that were made to the press or the military were usually fairly vague. People reported seeing saucer-shaped objects flying very fast, or bright lights at night moving around in unusual ways. On August 19, 1947, for instance, a Mr. and Mrs. Busby were sitting on the porch of their house in Butte, Montana, enjoying the warm evening. According to them, a large bright object suddenly flew overhead, heading northeast at a tremendous speed. Ten minutes later, so they claimed, another ten objects came over, flying rather slower, but again heading

UFO Files
ARE UFOS REAL?

The witnesses whose stories have been told in this chapter probably believed they were telling the truth, and thought they really did experience a visitation from another planet. But could their senses have been deceiving them? They might have misidentified astronomical objects such as clouds, planets, bright stars, meteors, artificial satellites, or the Moon. A number of UFO reports have been explained by flights of secret aircraft, weapons, and weather balloons, or by light phenomena such as mirages and searchlights. Other UFO stories have been the product of deliberate hoaxes. However, there remains a significant percentage of UFO sightings that cannot be explained.

northeast. According to the startled witnesses, three of the objects peeled off from the triangular formation and headed due north. It certainly took them by surprise.

29

The UFOs Arrive

On the morning of June 24, 1947, Kenneth Arnold, an experienced American aviator, set off from Chehalis, Washington, to his home in Oregon in his single-engine Callier light aircraft. With both time and fuel to spare, he decided first to spend an hour or so over the Mount Rainier area searching for a US military transport aircraft that had been reported missing and was presumed to have crashed. It was while turning on to a new leg of his search pattern at an altitude of 2,800 m (9,200 ft) that Arnold's alleged encounter began. The following is a description of what Arnold claimed happened next …

Arnold's Encounter

A bright flash of light swept over his aircraft. Such a thing usually happened when the Sun reflected off the surfaces of another aircraft close by. Fearing a collision with an aircraft he had not seen, Arnold scanned the skies, desperately seeking another plane. He soon saw a DC4 airliner some miles distant and flying away from him. Discounting this as the source of the flash, he then saw a second flash far to the north.

Staring at the location of the flash, Arnold saw a line of nine aircraft flying toward him at an angle. As the aircraft came closer, he saw that they were flying in echelon, a usual military formation, but arranged with the lead aircraft above the others, contrary to the standard military practice. Arnold at this point assumed that the fast-approaching aircraft were military jets of some kind, and relaxed. But as the nine aircraft came closer, Arnold was able to see them in detail and knew at once that he was seeing something very strange indeed.

Each aircraft was shaped like a wide crescent with neither fuselage nor tail. Moreover, the aircraft were flying with a strange undulating motion quite unlike the straight-line flight of all known aircraft. They also fluttered or dipped from side to side at times, sending off bright flashes as the Sun reflected from their highly polished, silver-blue surfaces. There were no markings that Arnold could see, though he was now concentrating hard on the mysterious aircraft. The formation was moving fast. Arnold timed it as it passed over landmarks what he had seen. Other pilots and air crew joined the conversation, but none could explain what Arnold had seen, other than to guess that the strange aircraft were some kind of secret military project. Still confused, Arnold then resumed his interrupted flight home to Oregon.

This artwork, signed by Kenneth Arnold, shows the aircraft he claimed to have seen. Arnold himself appears bottom left.

The Flying Saucer as I saw it... by Kenneth Arnold
Per copy 50¢

on the ground and later estimated the speed at around 2,100 kph (1,300 mph). This was much faster than any known aircraft of the time. Even military fast jets flew at only around 1,100 kph (700 mph). The aircraft were soon out of sight.

Secret Military Craft?

Arnold headed for Yakima Airfield and went to see Al Baxter, the general manager of Central Aircraft. The two men discussed the sighting, and Arnold drew pictures of

TALE OF THE PARANORMAL

TWO SHADOWS

Arnold's experience prompted others to come forward with their own stories. A group of boys from Baradine, Australia, were rabbiting by moonlight one night in 1931 when one of them—according to his later report—experienced something very unusual. The first thing he noticed, he said, was that he was casting two shadows. Looking up, he saw a disk-shaped object as bright as the Moon approaching from the northwest. Orange lights or flames flashed around its rim and the object rotated slowly as it flew. It followed a straight course before disappearing behind nearby hills.

By the time he arrived home, Arnold had begun to worry that he had seen some sort of highly advanced Soviet war machine. He decided to inform the FBI, but their office was closed, so he dropped in at the offices of the *East Oregonian* newspaper. He told the reporters there all about his experience. One of them, Bill Bequette, queried the way the unusual craft moved. Arnold elaborated on the undulating motion by saying, "They flew like a saucer would if you skipped it across water."

Bequette filed his report with a national news agency, writing about "flying saucers." It was repeated across America and soon the public was agog at news of these flying saucers. Meanwhile, Arnold had returned to the FBI to tell them about the strange aircraft. The local FBI man passed the details on to the head office in Washington, concluding his report with the words, "It is the personal opinion of the interviewer that Arnold actually saw what he states he saw in the attached report." Already concerned about Russian intentions and military technology, the US military pounced on Arnold's report. An era was born.

Eating His Words

News of Arnold's sighting spread quickly through aviation circles, leading to intense speculation. On July 4, 1947, a lunchtime discussion among airline staff at Boise Airport was cut short by United Airlines pilot E. J. Smith, who declared flatly that it was all nonsense.

TALE OF THE PARANORMAL

SIGHTING AT SNAKE RIVER CANYON

Some of the reports made in the wake of Arnold's sighting were clearly misidentified natural events. A glowing disk-shaped flying object seen over Codroy in Newfoundland turned out to be a meteorite heated red-hot by air friction as it crashed through the atmosphere. Others were more difficult to explain. For example, Mr. A.C. Urie and his two young sons claimed that on August 15, 1947, they saw a disk flying low over Snake River Canyon in Idaho while they were on a fishing trip. The object, they said, passed them at a distance of just 90 m (300 ft) and though it was moving extremely fast, all three apparently got a good look. It was about 6 m (20 ft), 3 m (10 ft) wide, and 3 m (10 ft) high. The object had a flange or rim around its base and made a soft whishing noise as it passed. As it rose out of the canyon, the object flew low over a line of poplar trees, which bent and twisted as if caught in a sudden, violent wind.

"I'll believe them when I see them," he finished, slamming down his newspaper and striding off to get his aircraft ready for flight. Smith took off and barely 20 minutes later allegedly found himself confronted by five disk-shaped flying objects, each of which was larger than his own DC3 airliner. The co-pilot and stewardess also claimed to have seen the objects before they flew off at high speed.

The Roswell Incident

Just two weeks after Arnold's sighting, the press officer, Walter Haut, at Roswell Air Force Base in New Mexico issued a dramatic press release. He said a flying saucer had crashed near the base and that air force personnel were investigating the debris. The press pounced on the story, expecting that the mystery of the flying saucers would soon be solved. Later that same day, however, a rather embarrassed Major Jesse Marcel called a press conference to announce that the crashed flying saucer was, in fact, a weather balloon of a new type that the Roswell men had not identified.

Fate *magazine, launched in 1948, led its first edition with the Arnold sighting.*

Astronomers Get in on the Act

It was not only aviators who were encountering flying saucers. On August 20, 1949, no less a figure than Clyde Tombaugh, the astronomer who had discovered Pluto, got involved in the growing mystery of flying saucers. At 10:45 PM he was sitting outside his house at Las Cruces, New Mexico, with his wife and her mother. His eye was caught, so he later said, by a green light flying overhead. According to Tombaugh, he looked up and saw seven other lights, all of the same green and all flying a parallel course. He thought that he could just make out a dark shape behind the lights, as if they were windows or lights attached to a large, unlit aircraft, but he could not be certain. The craft made no sound as it powered overhead and vanished into the distance.

On May 20 the following year, another astronomer saw a flying saucer. This was Dr. Seymour Hess of the Lowell Observatory at Flagstaff, Arizona. So Hess said, he was outside the observatory checking cloud cover when he spotted a bright object in

The astronomer Clyde Tombaugh sights eight mysterious green lights in the sky over his house in the Arizona desert in 1949.

the sky. He studied it through his binoculars for some seconds as it flew past. He later described the object as a shiny disk that was flying through thin cloud, sometimes disappearing behind the cloud and at other times flying beneath it. After a few seconds, the object flew out of sight.

Dogfight off Long Island

On October 29, 1952, two F94 jet fighters were patrolling off Long Island, New York. The F94 was not only heavily armed and fast, but had air-to-air radar operated by a second crew member sitting behind the pilot. The two aircraft were piloted by Lieutenant Burt Deane and Lieutenant Ralph Corbett. According to Deane, at about 2 AM he saw a bright white light ahead of the jets at an estimated 13 km (8 miles) distance. The following account is based on their own description of what happened next.

Aware that they were the first fast fighters to get this close to a flying saucer, Deane and Corbett decided to attack. Corbett got a radar lock first, but it was Deane who pushed his fighter to full power to close in for the attack. At once, the UFO began to move quickly, cutting inside the curve of Deane's turn. Deane pulled his fighter into its tightest possible turn, almost blacking out due to the extreme g-force, but he could not match the performance of the mystery aircraft. Corbett now came up to the attack, using standard fighter tactics to try to push the UFO into range of Deane's guns. It was to no avail. Whatever the pilots tried, the UFO managed to slip aside at the last moment—often at

speeds or performing turns quite impossible for the pursuing F94 fighters.

After about 10 minutes of dogfighting, the UFO climbed steeply away at supersonic speed. Deane and Corbett gave chase but were rapidly outpaced. The investigators who questioned the two pilots about the incident put it down as "unexplained."

Project Blue Book

The USAF eventually decided that the continuing flow of eyewitness reports of UFOs demanded some sort of response. In March 1952, Captain Edward J. Ruppelt was put in charge of the Air Technical Intelligence Center (ATIC), the section tasked with collecting and studying UFO reports. Ruppelt's task was given the code name Project Blue Book.

Close Encounters

On March 6, 1957, at about 2 PM, a woman in Trenton, New Jersey, was clearing up her back room when she heard her dog barking in the backyard. According to her later statement, she went out to see what was causing the fuss and saw the dog barking excitedly and looking up at a round flying object. Thus far, this represents a standard UFO sighting. What made it more valuable to UFO researchers was the fact that the alleged object was seen in broad daylight at close quarters, enabling the woman to make a detailed description of the UFO and its movements. This type of sighting would later come to be classified as a "close encounter of the first kind," or CE1 (see panel).

UFOs are consistently described by witnesses as having a disk shape, with a central raised dome.

The woman phoned her husband, who advised her to write it all down while it was still fresh in her mind. She described it as follows: the object was 150 m (500 ft) away and about 15 m (50 ft) across. It was shaped like a bowler hat. The central domed area was about 9 m (30 ft) high with steep sides while the flat bottom extended to form a rim about 5 m (15 ft) wide. The object looked to be made of a smooth but dull off-white substance. As the woman watched, the object began to sway slightly from side to side. A low rumbling noise began that grew louder, then faded only to become louder again. There then came a soft whooshing noise and the object disappeared into the clouds.

The woman sent her account to the USAF, where it was quietly filed away in Project Blue Book. Her account bore similarities to many other reports of sightings in terms of the shape of the object and its wobbling or rocking motion.

Spinning Disk

In 1980 bus conductor Russel Callaghan was on his usual route through the Yorkshire countryside near Bradford. Having reached the end of the journey, Callaghan and his driver halted the bus for a few minutes before the return trip. As they sat having a conversation on the grass the two men allegedly spotted a silver disk hovering over Emley Moor about 200 m (650 ft) away. The disk, they later said, began to spin, gaining speed, and then began to move. It gathered speed quickly and streaked out of view in about eight seconds.

UFO Files

CLASSIFYING UFO SIGHTINGS

In 1972, Dr. J. Allen Hynek devised a classification system for UFO sightings. The system comprises so-called "encounters" (UFOs seen at a distance) and "close encounters." A "close encounter of the first kind" (CE1) is when a UFO is seen at close quarters and for a fairly prolonged period of time. The witness is able to give a detailed description of the UFO, its shape, appearance, and actions.

A "close encounter of the second kind" (CE2) is essentially similar to a CE1, but where the UFO has some clear impact on its surroundings. This might be as simple as causing vegetation to sway as it passes, or may involve burning plants or ground with what appear to be engine blasts. A key feature is that the effect must be unique. To take an example, if a UFO is seen to land and marks are afterward found where the UFO rested, these marks should be unique and not identical to marks left by farm machinery nearby. Some UFO investigators collect samples of burnt grass and disturbed soil in the hope that analysis may reveal something about the motive power or composition of the UFO that affected them.

A "close encounter of the third kind" (CE3) occurs when a CE1 or CE2 is combined with the appearance of what seem to be occupants or crew from the UFO.

Photographic Evidence

Another CE1 took place in January 1958 when a Brazilian survey ship, the *Almirante Saldanha*, arrived at the Brazilian naval base on the Pacific island of Trinidade. Just after noon on the 16th, photographer Almiro Barauna was on deck when, it is claimed, another crew member pointed out to him an object in the sky. Barauna at first took the object to be an aircraft, but its lack of wings made him reach for his camera. The object circled around the island, then flew off. Before it did so, Barauna managed to take four photos.

The Trinidade sighting is famous largely because of the photos that were taken. The UFO shows features that are commonly mentioned in reports of sightings. The shape of a flattened sphere with a rim is one that crops up in a great many cases. That apart, the actions of the UFO were not particularly noteworthy. It apparently flew at a speed easily attained by conventional aircraft and its flight path, circling the island and heading off in a straight line, could be mimicked by a human craft. Were it not for the photos, skeptics might have dismissed this sighting as that of a misidentified aircraft.

Knowing that there must be no suspicion of fraud or hoaxing, Barauna persuaded the captain of the ship to supervise the developing of the photos in

This is one of the famous photos taken by Almiro Barauna of a "UFO" sighted from the Brazilian ship Almirante Saldanha *in 1958.*

the on-board laboratory, and on the ship's return to port he submitted the negatives and prints to the Brazilian navy for expert study.

In his excitement, Barauna had not checked the settings on the camera and all four pictures were consequently slightly over-exposed. Nevertheless, the craft could be seen to be a flattened sphere with a wide rim or flange around its middle, giving a rather Saturn-like appearance. The body of the craft was pale, the rim was dark, and a greenish mist or spray trailed behind it. The overall diameter of the craft was estimated to be 40 m (130 ft), and its speed around 950 kph (600 mph).

About a hundred sailors and residents at the base also apparently saw the UFO, and the developed photos matched exactly the descriptions given by several of these witnesses.

TALE OF THE PARANORMAL
LIKE AN OLD ZEPPELIN

A cigar-shaped object was allegedly seen over South Australia in July 1960 by a cook, Mrs. W. Pettifor, while she was walking to the hotel where she worked. She claimed she saw what looked at first to be an old Zeppelin airship, though she could not imagine what such a thing was doing there. The object seemed to glow orange as if there was some bright light deep within it. The object glided through the air in silence for a while, then halted for a few seconds before accelerating vertically at great speed and vanishing from sight.

Chase Over Portage County

On the night of April 16, 1966, Deputy Sheriffs Dale Spaur and Wilbur Neff were out on patrol in Portage County, Ohio. They were driving along Route 224 when they saw an abandoned wrecked car by the roadside and stopped to investigate. While Neff waited beside the police car, Spaur walked over to the wreck. Spaur inspected the car, concluded that nobody was around, and turned to go back to the police car. The following is based on descriptions by Spaur, Neff, and other witnesses of what happened next …

Spaur claimed he saw a large, brightly lit object coming toward them. He told Neff to turn around, which he did before freezing in alarm. The object was getting closer, and could now be seen to be about 12 m (40 ft) tall. It was emitting a quiet humming sound. The glowing object pulsated with various lights bright enough to illuminate the surrounding area. It was shaped like a football standing upright, though the top was more rounded and domed than the more pointed bottom. The object hovered over the police car for a few minutes at a height of about 250 m (800 ft), then moved off east. Spaur and Neff gave chase in their car.

They were later joined by Officer Wayne Huston, who was parked up on Route 14 when the UFO came flashing past, chased by Spaur and Neff. The object halted again near the village of Harmony. The three policemen stopped and got out of their cars to watch the UFO as it hung in the air, then climbed up at speed and disappeared from view. Before it disappeared, the object was also allegedly seen by a fourth policeman, Patrolman Frank Panzanella.

The key point about the Portage County sighting is that the object was seen at close quarters and from various angles over a considerable period of time by four different witnesses.

EYEWITNESS ACCOUNT

FRANK PANZANELLA'S STORY

I saw two other patrol cars pull up and the officers (Neff, Spaur, and Huston) got out of the car and asked me if I saw it. I replyed (sic) SAW WHAT! Then pointed at the object and I told them that I had been watching it for the last 10 minutes. The object was the shape of a half of (a) football, was very bright, and was about 8–11 m (25–35 ft) in diameter. The object then moved out toward Harmony Township approximately 300 m (1,000 ft) high, then it stopped then went straight up real fast to about 1,070 m (3,500 ft).

Encounter in Western Australia

Australian farmer A. Pool was driving back to his farm after a long day tending sheep on his station in Western Australia. Pool was trundling across a grassy paddock in his off-road vehicle when he spotted an aircraft about 800 m (2,625 ft) away heading toward him. Thinking a pilot was in trouble, he braked to a halt to await events. According to Pool, the approaching aircraft turned out to be a dull silver disk flying at about 120 m (420 ft) above the ground and heading downward. When he switched off his engine, he heard a loud whine similar to an electric motor running at high speed, coming from what he could now tell was no ordinary aircraft.

The object continued to dive until it came to a halt, hovering about 2 m (6 ft) from the ground and barely 3 m (10 ft) from Pool's car. He sat staring at the object, noticing that it had a flat underside and domed topside. The object was some 6 m (20 ft) across and at one end had a sort of upward bulge, which Pool took to be a cabin. There was what seemed to be a window on one side, but he could not see through it.

After sitting in amazement for some seconds, Pool decided to get out of his car and approach the strange object. No sooner had he opened the door, however, than the disk rocked to one side, then shot off at high speed.

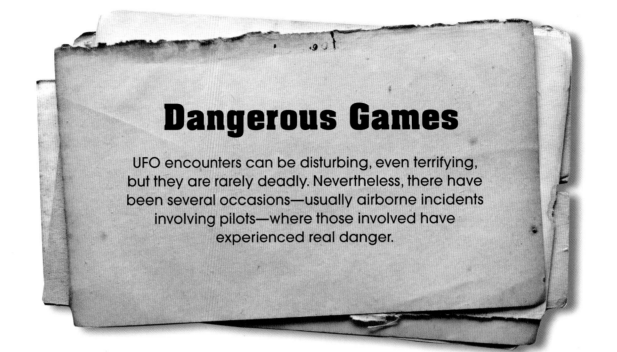

Dangerous Games

UFO encounters can be disturbing, even terrifying, but they are rarely deadly. Nevertheless, there have been several occasions—usually airborne incidents involving pilots—where those involved have experienced real danger.

The Gorman Dogfight

One of the best documented early examples of this took place on October 1, 1948. At 9 PM, 26-year-old Lieutenant George Gorman of the Air National Guard was on a routine practice flight in an F51 fighter. He was at an altitude of about 1,400 m (4,500 ft) and approaching Fargo Airport, North Dakota, ready to land, when he claimed he spotted a light moving below him.

Gorman thought that he was looking at the tail light of another aircraft and estimated it to be about 1,000 m (3,500 ft) beneath him, flying on a roughly parallel course at around 400 kph (250 mph). Worried that another aircraft was on his landing flight path, Gorman called up Fargo air traffic control, manned by L. D. Jensen. Jensen replied that the only other aircraft in the area was a Piper Cub, a

safe distance to the west. Gorman looked, and located the Cub. Looking back at the mystery light, Gorman watched as it flew over a floodlit football ground

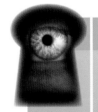

EYEWITNESS ACCOUNT

"I COULDN'T CATCH THE THING"

Gorman later related: "I dived after it at full speed (about 650 kph (400 mph) in an F51) but I couldn't catch the thing. I put my 51 into a sharp turn and tried to cut it off. By then we were at about 2,100 m (7,000 ft). Suddenly it made a sharp right turn and we headed straight at each other. Just when we were about to collide, I guess I lost my nerve. I went into a dive and the light passed over my canopy. Then it made a left circle about 300 m (1,000 ft) above and I gave chase again."

and was astonished to see that it was not attached to an aircraft but was seemingly a flying globe of light.

Alerted by Gorman, Jensen contacted Manuel Johnson in the control tower. Johnson claimed he took out his binoculars and located the light, confirming that it was not attached to an aircraft. Jensen peered into the sky and he, too, said he saw the odd light. Dr. A. Cannon and Einar Nelson in the Cub also claimed to see it, once he had been alerted by radio to the unfolding drama.

When the mystery light turned and began a dive toward the airport, Gorman decided to act. He was, after all, in the National Guard and flying in a fighter aircraft. He decided to give chase, but could not keep pace with it. The object then made a sharp turn and began heading straight for Gorman. At the last moment, he dipped his plane and the light passed overhead.

This time, Gorman decided, he would not pull out of any collision. Indeed he was quite prepared to ram the mystery object and radioed his intention to Fargo. Jensen and Johnson had by now abandoned their tasks and were able to follow the extraordinary dogfight that followed.

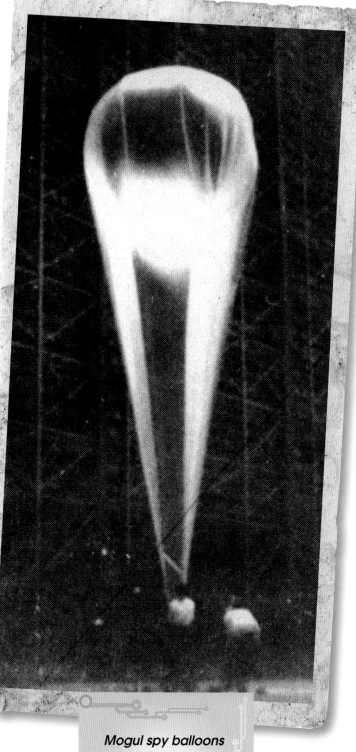

Mogul spy balloons like this one were used to spy on Soviet weapons tests and were highly classified.

For some 20 minutes Gorman and the mystery light chased each other around the sky over Fargo. Then the intruder seemed to tire of the proceedings. The light began a steep climb. Gorman followed it up to 5,200 m (17,000 ft), but was unable to keep up. The object flew off to the northwest at high speed. Gorman landed and filed a report.

Two Red Lights

On another occasion, a UFO apparently "buzzed" a passenger jet, forcing it to make an emergency landing. The Supercaravelle twin-engined jet liner of the Spanish airline TAE was flying from Salzburg to Tenerife on November 11, 1979. The pilot, Lerdo de Tejada, claimed that at around 11 PM he saw two bright red lights off to port at about the same altitude as his own aircraft, 7,500 m (24,000 ft). As the lights gradually approached, Tejada perceived that they were fixed to a rather larger flying object.

Due to the dark sky and darkness of the object, Tejada could not get a clear idea of the thing's shape or size. Following international procedure, Tejada called up Barcelona Air Control, in whose area he was, to report that a second aircraft was close to his. Barcelona confirmed that they had a second aircraft on their radar screens but that they could not identify it. Tejada decided to alter course to stay clear of the intruder, then return to his path toward Tenerife.

EPISODE OVER BRAZIL

Another Supercaravelle passenger jet was involved in a sighting over Brazil on May 7, 1967. The pilot and co-pilot both claimed to spot a disk-shaped aircraft ahead of them as they approached Porto Alegre. The disk was off-white with a row of flashing red lights around its rim. The aircraft's course would take it past the object with plenty of room to spare, but the co-pilot kept the disk in view. As the airliner drew level with it the disk began to move, falling in beside the aircraft at a distance of about 500 m (1,600 ft) and keeping pace with it. After about 20 minutes the object altered course, accelerated sharply, and disappeared into the distance.

Scary Dance

As he began the turn, however, the two red lights suddenly accelerated and climbed. They were now about 750 m (2,500 ft) from the airliner and began a bizarre dance around the TAE plane. One minute they were following the airliner, the next they were immediately above it, then they swooped down below.

Tejada was by now alarmed. The strange aircraft seemed to be playing games with him, and very dangerous games at that. When the red lights swooped down into the path of the Supercaravelle, Tejada had to haul his aircraft round in a sudden, tight turn to avoid a collision.

Emergency Landing

Tejada at once radioed Air Control and demanded to have permission for an emergency landing at the nearest available airport. He was directed to Manises Airport in Valencia, Spain, which was alerted to the approach of not only the jet but also the unidentified intruder. The TAE aircraft was followed to the airport by the UFO. The staff at the airport claimed that as Tejada landed, they saw that it was followed down by a large craft with two red lights. Seen from the ground the UFO was estimated to be as large as a Boeing 747. Once the passenger jet was on the ground, the UFO apparently streaked away at high speed.

The UFOs Land

The earliest reports of UFO sightings, and the majority of reports since, have been of flying objects seen mostly from a distance but sometimes from close up. Convincing as many people found these reports, they left behind them no evidence beyond the sightings themselves. Skeptics point out that the witnesses could have mistaken ordinary objects for something extraordinary, or that they might have been hallucinating or even lying.

Close Encounters of the Second Kind

However, during the 1950s, sightings began to be reported where the UFO apparently left behind physical traces of its passing. This could be anything from car engines cutting out to more bizarre effects such as the bending of light beams. In the terminology adopted by UFO researchers, these are close encounters of the second kind, or CE2s. They are quite rare, but extremely valuable to UFOlogists, as they allow them to learn a lot more about the UFO phenomenon.

The formation of crop circles is one of the most commonly reported instances of UFOs leaving evidence of their passage.

WHY ARE CE2s SO USEFUL TO UFOLOGISTS?

Sightings alone, even from believable witnesses offering detailed reports, are open to all sorts of doubts. The actual size of an observed object depends very much on how far away it was when seen, and judging distances can be notoriously difficult, especially at night or when seeing an object in the air. If an object leaves physical traces, however, these can be precisely measured and studied at leisure. Moreover, the type of traces left may indicate how the object moved, how hot it was, and of what material it was composed. For instance, holes cut from soil indicate a mechanical action, while holes burned in vegetation suggest radiant heat. They also make less likely the possibility that the witness invented or hallucinated the encounter.

Engine Failure

An early CE2 that achieved widespread publicity occurred on the night of November 2, 1957, at Levelland, Texas. The fact that this took place just an hour after the Russians had launched the world's second artificial satellite probably had something to do with the publicity the incident received.

At 11 PM Patrolman A. J. Fowler answered the phone at the Levelland police station. The call was from a man named Pedro Saucedo. Fowler could tell from Saucedo's voice that he was in some distress. Saucedo reported that his truck had broken down after he saw a bright light in the sky, but that it was now working again. Unable to get many details from Saucedo and thinking the man might have been drinking, Fowler logged the call but took no action.

But Fowler was in for a busy night. About an hour after logging Saucedo's call, he took a second call from a Mr. Watkins. This caller reported seeing an object shaped like an elongated egg, about 60 m (200 ft) long, resting on the road a few miles east of Levelland. Watkins said that as he approached the strange object, his car engine had stopped and his lights had gone out. A few seconds later the object took off and headed north. The car headlights had then come on and the engine was able to restart.

Fowler had barely hung up when he received a third call from a man reporting an almost identical incident north of Levelland. A fourth call followed from a terrified truck driver northeast of Levelland. Three more calls were made the following morning, making a total of seven motor vehicles that spluttered to a stop after encountering a UFO that night.

By 1 AM, Fowler had alerted all local police vehicles to the bizarre reports he was receiving. Patrolmen Lee Hargrove and Floyd Gavin reported a sighting of the UFO at a distance, but said it was moving too fast for them to catch it. Fire Marshal Ray Jones picked up the police radio reports and drove out to join the UFO hunt. He, too, claimed to see the UFO and, although his engine promptly spluttered, it did not stop.

Once the local newspaper printed the story, over 50 local residents came forward to say that they had seen a strange light or object in the skies around Levelland that night.

Encounter in Tasmania

A broadly similar experience occurred on the evening of September 22, 1974, near Launceston, Tasmania. A woman, known as Mrs. W. in press reports, drove to an out-of-town bus stop where she was due to pick up a visiting relative, parked her car, and settled down to listen to the radio.

After a few minutes, she said, the radio began to emit a high-pitched whine. Mrs. W. reported that as she bent forward to fiddle with the radio controls she saw that the land around her car was slowly being illuminated by a whitish light. Looking up to see the source of the light the woman apparently saw a UFO approaching at a height of about 15 m (50 ft).

The object was about as big as a truck.

The top half consisted of a curved dome that was pulsating with a bright orange-red light. The underside was shaped more like an inverted cone, though with distinct horizontal banding. The lower half was dark silver and was emitting a pale whitish light.

Unsurprisingly the woman decided to get away as quickly as possible. She started her engine, put the car into reverse, and accelerated away as the UFO reached within 30 m (100 ft) of her car. The car had gone barely 100 m (330 ft) when it ran off the road and the engine cut out.

Hair Straightener

Mrs. W. watched in alarm as the UFO approached, then came to a halt. It then bobbed off to its left before climbing steeply into the sky and vanishing into clouds.

As soon as the UFO was out of sight, Mrs. W. leapt from the car and ran home. Her husband met her at the door and, having calmed her down enough to get the story from her, noticed that her hair, which had been permed a few days earlier, was now straight again.

Next morning, Mr. W. walked up the road to retrieve the car with his son. They started the vehicle without trouble, but were deeply puzzled by the fact that the front half of the car was gleaming clean, while the rear half was as dirty as it had been when Mrs. W. had begun her ill-fated journey.

Somehow the UFO had not only interfered with the car radio—which apparently never again worked properly—it had also seemingly straightened Mrs. W's hair and cleaned the paintwork on her car.

UFOs are often sighted near roads. Some observers claim that their advanced technology is able to remotely override the engines of cars.

Bending Beams

Rather more bizarre than simply switching them off was the effect on the headlights of a car near Bendigo in Victoria, Australia, on the night of April 4, 1966. Ronald Sullivan was driving along a straight rural road in a remote area near Bendigo when the beams sent out by the headlights of his car apparently began bending to the right.

Understandably puzzled, he braked to a halt, intending to inspect his headlights. Sullivan said that as he got out of his car, he noticed a round or domed object in a field off the road in the direction toward which the headlight beams were bending. The object was of indistinct shape and glowed with various, shifting shades, most noticeably red and blue. The object then rose into the air and flew off, after which the headlights returned to normal.

Glowing Sphere

If the stories are true, UFO-induced power failures do not only affect simple circuits such as those controlling car ignitions and headlights. On the evening of October 20, 1990, a much more dramatic electrical power breakdown occurred in the Botosani region of Romania.

At around 10 pm that evening, Virgil Atodiresei was walking home to his farm near Flaminzi. According to his later testimony, he saw a light glowing through clouds over the nearby village of Poiana, but at first took no real notice of it. Then, so

GRAVEYARD ENCOUNTER

One sighting that had a direct effect on the witness took place at Leominster, Massachusetts, on March 8, 1967. A couple were driving home just after midnight when they drove past the town cemetery. They later reported seeing a light and a trail of smoke in the cemetery and stopped to investigate. The man got out of the car intending to enter the cemetery to see if something was on fire. As he did so the bright light began to rise slowly from the ground, moving silently and smoothly.

The man put out his arm to point at the rising object and called out to his wife to look. Then several things happened at once. First, the car's engine cut out, as did the headlights, radio, and dashboard lights. Secondly, the man felt a mild electric shock run through his body and his outstretched arm was pulled down to slam hard onto the roof of the car. The man tried desperately to pull his arm free, but it seemed to be glued to the vehicle.

The rising object then began to emit a loud humming sound and to rock from side to side. As the object gathered speed and moved away, the car lights came back on. The man found he could move again, and wasted no time in starting the engine and driving away as fast as he could.

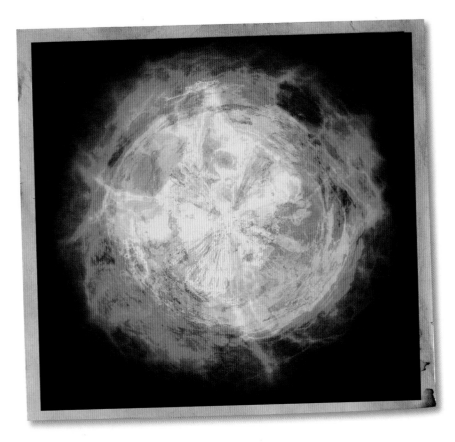

he claimed, he saw an almost spherical object descend from the clouds. It had a slightly indistinct outline, but glowed as if there were several bright lights moving around within an opaque globe. Atodiresei could see it was big, but could not estimate its precise size.

Meanwhile, all the lights in Poiana went out as the electrical supply failed. Power cuts in rural Romania were not unusual, so most villagers simply went to bed. However, Professor Nicolai Bildea had his students' mathematical papers to mark. He had a lantern in an outside shed and so went out into the backyard to find it. As he left his house he noticed a flickering yellow-red light. Thinking that a nearby barn or haystack might have caught fire despite the persistent drizzle, Bildea went out into the street to investigate.

Energy Consumer

Bildea later claimed that as he came around the corner of his house, he saw a large object shaped like a tortoise shell, about 50 m (160 ft) long and 12 m (40 ft) wide. Around the edge of the flat lower side he could see a number of small white lights. From four of these, beams of light were pointing down and sweeping the village. One swept over him briefly and was extremely bright. The rain had by now stopped, so Bildea ran back to get his wife and mother to see the UFO. By the time they reached the street the UFO was moving off and they got only a distant view of it. As the UFO left, the rain began again, this time a heavy downpour rather than the earlier drizzle. Half an hour or so later the electricity supply came back on.

Chapter 3

Alien Encounters

Since the late 1940s there have been abundant reports from all over the world of strange figures being seen in, beside, and close to UFOs. Most of these accounts do not provide much information as to what the alleged aliens are actually doing here. They come and go, but it is hard to say why. However, there have been some reported instances of aliens interacting with humans, and, if these reports are to be believed, they may offer clues about the aliens' intentions. The fact that the reports tend to be inconsistent and often contradictory leads many Ufologists to conclude that there is more than one type of alien.

Encounter Near Hasselbach

In 1952 a German official named Oscar Linke was riding his motorbike with his 11-year-old daughter Gabriella near Hasselbach when they got a puncture. As they walked along the road pushing the bike, Gabriella saw something in a clearing. She pointed it out to her father, who at first took it to be a group of deer in the long grass but then decided it wasn't. He left the road and went to investigate. The following is based on Linke's description of what happened next.

When he was about 30 m (100 ft) from the object, he saw two men dressed in silver suits who were bent over and fiddling with something on the ground. One of the men had a light attached to a belt around his waist.

Linke walked on until he was just 7.5 m (25 ft) from the men. He then saw, in a position where it was hidden from the road, a large circular object resting on the ground.

Linke estimated that it was about 15 m (50 ft) across and shaped like two frying pans placed rim to rim but without the handles. On top of the object was a cylindrical tower about

3 m (10 ft) tall. Around the rim of the object was a row of dull, yellowish lights, each one about a foot across and spaced some 60 cm (2 ft) apart.

Seeing her father stop in surprise, Gabriella asked him what was wrong. At the girl's voice, the two men looked up and saw Linke. They quickly jumped into an opening on the tower and disappeared from view. The lights on the object grew brighter and turned green as a hum began to emanate from it. The tower slid down into the object as the lights turned red and the hum grew louder.

The object began to rise, and when it reached a height just above the trees, the hum became a whistle that grew in pitch and intensity until it was almost unbearable. The object then flew off at great speed to the north.

Nordic Types

UFO researchers who have studied eyewitness descriptions of aliens have learned that most of the reported aliens fit into one of a small number of types. Among the first of these to be reported in any number are the Nordics. These aliens were given this name as they tend to be very humanlike and almost invariably tall with long blond hair and blue eyes, similar to the popular image of Scandinavians. They are usually seen dressed in one-piece, tight outfits that are described as being like ski suits or motorcycle leathers.

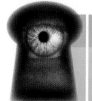

EYEWITNESS ACCOUNT

LINKE'S STATEMENT

"I would have thought that both my daughter and I were dreaming if it were not for the following element involved: When the object had disappeared, I went to the place where it had been. I found a circular opening in the ground and it was quite evident that it was freshly dug. It was exactly the same shape as the conical tower. I was then convinced that I was not dreaming."

The Nordics are generally reported to behave in an aloof or detached fashion. They stare at the humans who see them and sometimes seem to take notes or talk about the humans. Some witnesses report that the Nordics seem friendly. Reports of the Nordics were most frequent during the 1950s and 1960s, but they declined in number during the 1970s and have never really become numerous again.

Alien Files

TRICKSTERS

UFO researchers believe that the "Trickster" type of aliens are seen more often than either the Nordics or the Goblins. According to witnesses, these aliens appear to be broadly similar to humans, though they rarely stand more than 0.9 m (3 ft) tall. They are often said to wear one-piece suits and sometimes helmets or face masks. Tricksters are frequently reported to be deeply interested in plants and animals, especially crops or domestic livestock. They have allegedly been seen taking samples from plants and attempting to catch animals.

If witnesses are to be believed, the Tricksters, like the Nordics, seem somewhat uninterested in humans and react as if the arrival of a human is a bit of a nuisance. Sometimes they run away or take off in their UFO. At other times they will motion for the human witness to leave. If that does not work, they may freeze or incapacitate the human, often with a tool that emits a beam of light.

Goblin Types

Very different are the "Goblin" types. UFO experts say that these aliens are short, usually around 0.9–1.2 m (3–4 ft) tall. Although they are described as humanoid in that they walk upright on two legs and have two arms and one head, they are otherwise bizarre in appearance. According to witnesses, they generally have long arms that end in claws or talons, large heads with grotesquely pointed ears, and eyes that are reported to look evil or malevolent. Some Goblin types are reported to be covered in dense hair or long fur, but most are naked with smooth or reptilian skin.

The Goblin types are apparently as aggressive as their eyes would indicate. They are prone to attack humans, inflicting cuts and scratches, and sometimes seem intent on dragging humans into their spacecraft. They are usually, but not always, said to be much stronger than their size would suggest. According to most reports, there is a noticeable lack of any technology or implements when compared to other alien types. Perhaps fortunately, reported sightings of these Goblin types have always been rare.

Grays

Ufologists call the most common type of reported alien the Gray. According to witnesses, these beings stand just under 1.2 m (4 ft) tall and are humanoid in appearance. They have thin arms, legs, and bodies, but very large and rounded

heads. The arms and legs are sometimes said to lack elbows or knees and to end in long fingers and toes that are opposable but again lack clearly defined joints.

The heads are hairless and often earless and noseless. The mouths are usually described as being mere slits, if they are mentioned at all. It is the eyes that seem to be the most noticeable feature of this type of alien. They are invariably described as being extremely large, jet black, and almond-shaped. Some witnesses report them to have hypnotic powers, while others believe that any telepathic communication they receive is by way of these trance-inducing eyes.

The Grays are generally reported as unfriendly. Like the Tricksters, they sometimes take an interest in plants and animals, but unlike the Tricksters they are very interested in humans. Attacks by Grays are generally more sophisticated than the physical violence of the Goblins but are nonetheless disturbing. They will try to induce humans onto their craft for a variety of unpleasant purposes.

ALIEN CONTACT

Some people have claimed not only to have encountered the occupants of UFOs, but to have spoken with them. Sometimes the conversation allegedly takes place in the language of the human who encounters the beings; at other times it involves miming or some form of telepathic communication.

Mental Images

In October 1959, Gideon Johannson had a power outage at his rural house in Mariannelund, Sweden. He and his son went outside to see if there were any obvious problems and, according to their later report, saw an unusual flying object behaving in an odd manner. Shaped like a bell with a large window on one side and glowing white, the UFO rocked from side to side, changed direction abruptly, and crashed through the branches of a tree before coming to rest, hovering a short distance away.

Johannson went to investigate and was 3 m (10 ft) from the object when he suddenly noticed two humanoids through the window. He stopped abruptly when he became aware that the beings had also seen him. The figures were short with dome-shaped heads and pointed chins, but their main features were their eyes. These were large, dark, and beautiful.

One of the beings used its eyes to transfer mental images to Johannson. These urged him to stay where he was, and showed the figures doing work on their craft, apparently repairing it. Johannson did his best to communicate back by thought or by waving, but the aliens ignored him. After some minutes the UFO rose into the air, hovered and then emitted a bright flash, after which it was gone.

When the power engineers came to repair the power outage, they found that the lines leading to the Johannson house had been damaged about a mile away. Johannson believed that the UFO had inadvertently hit the cables, causing it to fly unpredictably and then come down to hover while the crew repaired the damage.

Alien Pancakes

Farmer Joe Simonton claimed to have achieved successful nonverbal communication with aliens during his alleged encounter with a UFO near his home at Eagle River in Wisconsin. The incident, which occurred on April 18, 1961, began as a fairly typical UFO close encounter. Simonton later said he heard a

rumbling sound and, on leaving his house to investigate, saw a silver oval craft about 9 m (30 ft) across and 3.7 m (12 ft) high, flying over his house.

The object came down to land a short distance away. Suddenly a hatch opened on top of the object, and three humanoid heads emerged. One of the figures climbed out. It was around 1.5 m (5 ft) tall and dressed in a tight-fitting outfit with a belt around the waist. The fabric was very dark blue, almost black, and seemed to be made of rubber or some such material. The creature's head was very human-looking with its straight, short black hair and swarthy complexion.

The alien had in his hand a large jug. He mimed as if drinking from the jug, from which Simonton concluded that his visitors were thirsty. He took the jug, filled it in his kitchen, and brought it back. As he handed over the jug, Simonton peeked into the craft through the hatch and saw one of the aliens apparently frying something in a pan over a sort of stove. Simonton pointed to the pan and mimed eating food. The alien

understood, picked up four pancake-like objects, and handed them over to Simonton. The alien then closed the hatch and the UFO flew off, leaving Simonton with the pancakes. The farmer phoned the local authorities, who passed the details on to the UFO researcher Dr. J. Allen Hynek.

By the time Hynek and his team made contact with Simonton, he had eaten one of the pancakes. It was, he said, fairly unpleasant, having a taste and consistency like that of cardboard.

Alien Files

WHAT WERE THE PANCAKES MADE OF?

Hynek sent one of the other pancakes off for analysis. This showed it to be made of wheat bran, soya bean husks, buckwheat hulls, and vegetable fats. In other words, it was from Earth.

57

Montana prospector Udo Wartena apparently gave permission for an alien to extract water from a mountain stream.

The following account is based on his description of what happened next.

Turning to face the direction of the noise, Wartena saw what he took to be a military aircraft. It was hovering about 180 m (600 ft) away, above a stream that meandered through a meadow. The craft was large. Wartena later estimated it to be about 30 m (100 ft) long and shaped like a lens, with the central section about 11 m (35 ft) thick.

"Just Like Us"

As Wartena watched, he saw a section of the hull drop down to reveal a spiral staircase. Down the stairs came a humanlike figure dressed in a uniform with a cap. The new arrival began approaching Wartena, so the prospector strolled forward. The figure waved at Wartena, and as they got to within 3 m (10 ft) of each other, he asked if it would be all right to take some water from the stream. Wartena said it was. The stranger then turned and waved back to his craft. A hose came down from the hovering UFO to dip into the stream.

Encounter in Montana

When the aliens show that they can speak the language of the witness, it makes communication much easier than with gestures and sign language. One such encounter apparently took place in May 1940, though it did not become public until some years later.

Udo Wartena was working on his small gold claim in a remote valley near Townsend, Montana, when—so he later claimed—he heard a loud rushing noise, like that of a turbine. He was familiar with the various army aircraft that flew overhead and assumed that this was one flying closer to the ground than usual.

The man then invited Wartena on board his craft. Still thinking that he was dealing with the US military, Wartena agreed. He climbed the spiral stairs to find himself in a room about 3.5 x 4.5 m (12 x 15 ft). The room was lit by a pale light, the source of which Wartena could not see.

In the room was an older man seated on a plushly padded bench. Wartena asked why the men wanted water from his small stream when there was a large lake not far away. The younger man replied that it was because the stream water was purer and contained no algae.

Wartena had now discovered that although the man spoke good American English, he was doing so slowly and stumbling over certain words as if this were not his native language. In May 1940, war was raging in Europe and Asia, and Wartena suddenly became suspicious of where these men were from, and so he asked them. "We are from a different planet," came the reply. "It is a long way from here." Wartena was surprised, to say the least, by this response but felt totally at ease with the aliens. They were "just like us, and very nice," he later reported.

Wartena asked his new alien friends why they had come to Earth. He was told that they had been visiting Earth for some years to gather information, leave instructions and help out when they could. They then invited Wartena to come with them, but he declined, saying that his friends and family relied on him and he could not just go wandering off without telling them.

Alien Files

SKIPPING OVER LIGHT WAVES

Wartena claimed that the younger alien explained to him how their craft worked. The alien said that there were two flywheels around the rim of the craft that spun in opposite directions. This gave the craft an internal gravity negating that of Earth or any other planet. The craft gained its power by focusing the gravitational energy of whatever celestial body was the closest and then using this to skip over the light waves faster than the speed of light. They claimed to be able to store small amounts of the gravitational energy for emergency use.

At this, the two men ushered Wartena off the UFO. They told him to get well away from the craft before it took off and not to discuss the event with anyone. In the event, Wartena did not move off far enough. The rushing noise began again, and the rim of the UFO began to spin. It lifted vertically off the ground, hovered for a few seconds while wobbling slightly, and then flew off. As it left, Wartena collapsed. His muscles simply would not work and did not return to normal for more than an hour.

Robots and Blobs

As well as humanoid aliens, other types have been reported that owe little or nothing to human anatomy. Robots are, perhaps, the most numerous of these beings. Ufologists say they tend to be of metallic appearance and often have flashing lights attached to their bodies. A final category goes by various names, such as "Exotic" or "Bizarre," depending on the researcher involved in classifying them. The category includes all sorts of odd and unusual alien reports. Some witnesses have seen disembodied brains, headless birdmen, or bouncing blobs of jelly. Most aliens in this category are only reported once.

Visitors from Cassiopeia

In September 1955, Josef Wanderka was riding his moped through woods near Vienna, Austria, when—so he later reported—he came upon a silvery egg-shaped object resting in a clearing. A

TALE OF THE PARANORMAL

FARM TALK

Gary Wilcox, a farmer from Newark in Newark Valley, New York, claimed that he found a strange object in one of his fields on April 24, 1964. Shaped rather like an elongated egg, about 6 m (20 ft) long and 1.2 m (4 ft) tall, it seemed to be made of a shiny, silver metal, all of one piece, without any signs of joints or rivets.

Wilcox apparently gave the object a kick. Suddenly two figures came out from underneath the object. They were about 1.2 m (4 ft) tall and dressed in white overalls that had a metallic sheen. Wilcox began backing away, but one alien called out to him, "Don't be alarmed, we have spoken to people before."

Wilcox later thought that although he could understand clearly what was being said, the figure had not actually been speaking English but had been making strange bubbling and moaning noises. The aliens asked Wilcox if he could explain how his tractor worked. Wilcox did so, and then he was asked what he was doing with it. He explained that he had been spreading manure on a field, but the aliens did not seem to understand the concept of fertilizer, so Wilcox went on to explain that as well.

The aliens said that their home planet was very rocky and unsuitable for growing Earth-type crops. They said that they preferred to visit rural areas as the skies over cities were too polluted with fumes and gases that interfered with their craft's energy system. The aliens then disappeared back under the object. The object rose slowly and silently to a height of about 45 m (150 ft) before gliding off to the north.

door in the side of the object was open, and a ramp led down to the grassy glade. Gingerly, Wanderka entered the object to find himself in a large, featureless room, where he was confronted by six humanoids.

The humanoids, according to Wanderka, were taller than him, and each had long blond hair tied back in a bun or ponytail. He likened their faces to those of children. They were dressed in one-piece garments that reached from the neck to the wrists and toes. Taken aback, Wanderka stammered out his profuse apologies for having entered the craft, introduced himself and began backing out of the door.

The aliens that farmer Gary Wilcox claims to have met were fascinated by his tractor.

One of the humanoids then began talking in German with a slight accent. It urged Wanderka not to leave, assuring him that he was in no danger. The alien said that they had come from the star system Cassiopeia and asked Wanderka how things were on Earth. This being the height of the Cold War, with Austria caught between the Soviet and capitalist areas, Wanderka blurted out a quick summary of the current international tensions.

The alien suggested that perhaps Wanderka could become Earth's leader and sort the problems out. Wanderka was wondering how to respond to this odd suggestion when the alien changed the subject and demanded to know how the moped worked. After Wanderka had explained, he was ushered out of the UFO, which then took off.

George Adamski

George Adamski was a Polish-born American citizen who shot to international fame in 1954 with the publication of his book *Flying Saucers Have Landed*. The book, co-written by British writer Desmond Leslie, was based for the most part on Adamski's alleged encounter with a UFO in 1952. Adamski asserted that on November 20 of that year, he and some friends had been enjoying a picnic in the Mojave Desert when they saw a large, cigar-shaped UFO pass overhead, chased by some military jets. As the UFO fled, a smaller disk-shaped UFO seemed to detach itself and came down to land a mile or so away. While his friends waited, Adamski set off to investigate the landed flying saucer. The following is based on Adamski's description of what happened next.

As he approached, he was met by a humanoid who was dressed in brown overalls. The alien could speak no English but made himself understood by a mixture of hand signals and telepathy. The being explained that he had come from the planet Venus as a messenger to Earth. The Venusians were a highly advanced culture but were deeply worried by the wrong turn that humanity had taken technologically by taking up nuclear power for both warlike and power-

These two photographs were taken by George Adamski. He claimed that they were evidence that alien spacecraft had visited Earth.

generating purposes. The Venusian said that not only was humanity at risk, but so were other interplanetary races, as the radiation was leaking out from Earth into space. The Venusian explained that he and his race wished to correct the path of humanity by peaceful means but warned that other races—from Jupiter, Saturn, and interstellar planets—were not so well disposed and might resort to force if mankind did not change its path voluntarily.

The Venusian then asked to borrow a roll of photographic film that Adamski had on him. Adamski handed it over, whereupon the alien left.

Adamski hurried back to his friends with his news. They agreed to sign a statement confirming their viewing of the original UFO and the smaller saucer.

On December 13, Adamski returned to the desert to retrieve his film. He was visited by a flying saucer, the film dropping from a porthole. When developed, it showed a variety of spacecraft.

Alien Files

WAS ADAMSKI A FRAUD?

The book and photographs created a sensation. Some believed Adamski; others condemned him as a charlatan. His background as part-time philosopher, self-appointed professor, one-time alcohol bootlegger, and burger-stand salesman did not inspire confidence.

In 1955 two of the friends who had been at the fateful picnic came forward to say that in fact they had seen no UFO. They had signed the statement prepared by Adamski to help him sell the story for cash, but now that the story was becoming so widely believed, they felt that they had to retract.

In the years that followed, Adamski claimed to have been visited by the Venusians on several more occasions. He also claimed to have been taken to the Moon and to Venus, where he found lush forested valleys. By 1960 his claims had become utterly outlandish and lacked any evidence to support them. The photos of spacecraft were proclaimed by experts to be clever fakes made by photographing detailed models in carefully controlled artificial light.

Adamski died in 1965. Soon afterward space probes would reveal that the planets he claimed to have visited were quite unlike his descriptions, and their environmental conditions made them incapable of supporting life, let alone advanced beings.

Men in Black

Some UFO witnesses claim that after their encounter they faced questions and threats from "men in black"—men, usually dressed in black suits who claim to be officials of secret institutions or government agents. They often threaten UFO witnesses to keep quiet about what they have seen. Some ufologists believe men in black are, in fact, aliens whose job is to prevent witnesses from talking about them.

One of the earliest reported men in black episodes took place in 1954 when UFO investigator Albert Bender was at home in Connecticut. Bender was head of the International Flying Saucer Bureau and published a regular journal titled *Space Review*. He claims he was visited by three men dressed in smart black business suits and wearing black, homburg-style hats. They kept the hats pulled down so that the brims partially hid their faces. One of them was carrying a copy of *Space Review*. After standing around in ominous silence for some time, the men began communicating with Bender by telepathic means. They told him that he had to stop his UFO investigations at once. They issued threats and made claims that terrified Bender.

The next day, Bender ceased publication of *Space Review* and resigned from the International Flying Saucer Bureau. He later moved to the West Coast of the US, cut off all contact with his friends and insisted on having an unlisted phone number. Thereafter several UFO witnesses, and some investigators, began reporting threatening visits from men dressed in black, or in official uniforms of one kind or another.

In November 1961, Paul Miller claims he saw a landed UFO and two humanoids in North Dakota. According to Miller, the following day he was visited in his office by three men in black suits who claimed to be from the government. They asked him detailed questions about the UFO and demanded to be shown the clothes that Miller had been wearing at the time. Miller was so frightened that he drove them to his house and showed them the clothes. After inspecting them, the men left.

Empty Threats

In 1967, Robert Richardson reported sighting a UFO near Toledo, Ohio. According to Richardson, he saw it land and later picked up a piece of metal from the landing site, which he passed to a scientist for analysis. Three days later—so he claims—two men pulled up outside his house in a 14-year-old black Cadillac. They asked him a few innocuous questions about the UFO and then left.

Alien Files

WHO ARE THE MEN IN BLACK?

Opinion is divided among UFO investigators as to who the men in black might be. Some ufologists believe men in black are in fact aliens, or androids controlled by aliens, sent out to cover up alien activity on Earth. Others think they are government agents seeking to hush up UFO sightings. A third theory is that they are hallucinations caused by the trauma of encountering a UFO. The truth is that nobody is entirely certain who the men in black might be. It is clear, however, that, as far as we know, none of their threats have ever been carried out and nobody has ever suffered at their hands.

A week later, says Richardson, two different men arrived in a different car. They wore black suits and spoke with foreign accents. They acted in a threatening fashion and sought to bully Richardson into accepting that the UFO sighting had been a mistake or dream. Then one of the men asked for the piece of metal. When Richardson said he no longer had it, the man turned angry. "If you want your wife to stay as pretty as she is, you had better get that metal back," the intruder declared. Then both men left the house hurriedly. It subsequently turned out that both cars had fake license plates and that the metal was a fairly nondescript iron alloy. The men were never seen again, and their threats were not carried out.

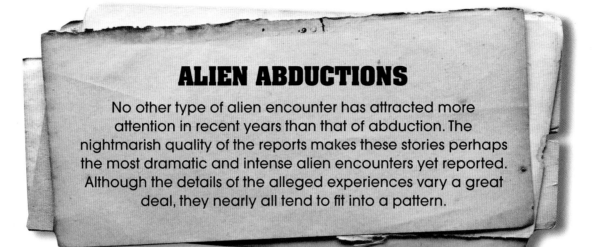

ALIEN ABDUCTIONS

No other type of alien encounter has attracted more attention in recent years than that of abduction. The nightmarish quality of the reports makes these stories perhaps the most dramatic and intense alien encounters yet reported. Although the details of the alleged experiences vary a great deal, they nearly all tend to fit into a pattern.

The Wolski Encounter

One morning in the summer of 1978, Jan Wolski, a 71-year-old Polish farmer, was driving his horse-drawn cart through the woods near his home. According to Wolski, on the road ahead of him, he suddenly saw two small humanoids. The beings, he later said, were about 1.2 m (4 ft) tall and very slender in build. They were dressed in tight-fitting, one-piece silvery outfits. Their heads were larger than a human's would have been in proportion to their bodies, and they had large, dark, almond-shaped eyes. Their ears and noses were very small and their mouths little more than slits. Bizarrely,

The creatures that Jan Wolski allegedly encountered had large heads and dark, almond-shaped eyes.

they were bouncing along as if their shoes contained hidden springs. The following account is based on Wolski's description of what happened next.

When Wolski came closer, the two creatures noticed him and bounded over to sit up on the cart. One of them pointed forward along the lane, seemingly indicating that Wolski should continue. The two beings then chatted to each other in a language that Wolski did not understand. He did, however, get the very strong impression that the beings were in a jovial and happy mood. After a few minutes the cart entered a clearing, and the two beings jumped down. They began bounding off toward a UFO that was hovering above the clearing. The object was white and shaped like a house, with a pitched roof like that of a barn. At each corner were cylindrical objects from which projected vertical black poles topped by spinning spiral objects. A loud and intense humming sound filled the air. As Wolski watched, a black box-like object began descending from the UFO on four cables.

Entering the UFO

One of the humanoids then turned to Wolski and beckoned him over. Since he had felt no impression of hostile intent, Wolski climbed down from his cart and walked across the clearing to the UFO. The being then gestured for him to enter the box, which he did. The box ascended into the UFO. Stepping out of the box, Wolski found himself inside a very gloomy room. There were two large tubes extending from one side of the UFO interior to the other, and a number of rods in the floor that Wolski took to be controls. Also on the floor were a dozen or so birds, apparently stunned or dead.

One of the humanoids indicated by hand signals that Wolski should lie down, which he did. The aliens then studied Wolski visually and passed what seemed to be scanners over his body. He was then instructed to stand up and was shown back to the box-like elevator apparatus. The elevator descended with Wolski and the two aliens in it. After Wolski exited the elevator, the UFO rose slowly into the air before departing at high speed.

Alien Files

WHAT ARE ALIEN ABDUCTIONS?

Alien abductions are experiences—real or imagined—in which people are taken against their will by apparently nonhuman entities and subjected to physical and psychological tests. The first case to gain widespread attention was that of Antonio Villas Boas, a Brazilian farmer, who claimed to have been abducted by aliens in 1957. Since then there have been many hundreds of alleged cases, particularly in the United States. Do they really happen? Most scientists believe that alien abductions are in fact a product of fantasy, false-memory syndrome, hallucination, hypnosis, and other psychological phenomena.

The Pascagoula Case

On the evening of October 11, 1973, two shipyard workers ran into the police station in Pascagoula, Mississippi, claiming that they had been abducted by aliens. Sheriff Fred Diamond did not at first believe a word of the story, but seeing that the men were clearly terrified, he agreed to take a statement. Both men, Charlie Hickson and Calvin Parker, told near-identical tales.

The men claimed they had been fishing from a pier in an isolated area off Highway 90. They had heard a loud zipping noise behind them and turned to see an oval-shaped object hovering about 0.9 m (3 ft) off the ground. The object was glowing with a pale blue light. A door opened in the side of the craft, and three humanoids came floating out. The figures were about 1.5 m (5 ft) tall and glowed with a soft white light. Their heads were high and domed with large, black eyes and slits for mouths. Their ears were small, conical, and stuck out sideways from their heads. Their arms ended in clawlike hands with simple pincers instead of fingers. Both Parker and Hickson said that they thought the beings were robots rather than living beings.

Charlie Hickson and Calvin Parker were fishing in the Mississippi when they were abducted by three strange-looking aliens.

One of the aliens grabbed Hickson by the shoulder, causing him to feel a strange stinging or tingling sensation. He then drifted into a trancelike state in which he was only vaguely aware of what was happening. Parker passed out completely at this point and was unable to remember anything.

According to Hickson, both men were levitated by the aliens and floated into the UFO. Inside the craft, the men were subjected to what appeared to be medical tests. Hickson recalled lying on a table while a gigantic scanning device shaped like an enormous eye was passed repeatedly over him.

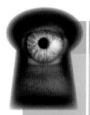

EYEWITNESS ACCOUNT

SECRET TAPE

After telling their story to Sheriff Diamond, Hickson and Parker were secretly taped to see if they were really telling the truth. Here is a transcript of part of their conversation.

Parker: I got to get home and get to bed or … or see the doctor or something. I can't stand it. I'm about to go half crazy.

Hickson: I tell you, when we're through, I'll get you something to settle you down so you can get some … sleep.

Parker, his voice rising: My … arms, my arms, I remember they just froze up and I couldn't move. Just like I stepped on a … rattlesnake.

Now both talk as if to themselves.

Parker: I passed out. I expect I never passed out in my whole life.

Hickson: I've never seen nothin' like that before in my life. You can't make people believe –

Parker: I don't want to keep sittin' here. I want to see a doctor –

Hickson: They better wake up and start believin' … they better start believin'.

"We Mean You No Harm"

The aliens then floated the two men back out to the riverbank and dumped them on the ground next to their abandoned fishing tackle. One of the beings then sent a telepathic message to Hickson, saying: "We are peaceful. We mean you no harm." Parker came to at this point, just in time to see the aliens leave and the UFO fly off.

By the time he had finished taking down the statement, Sheriff Diamond was skeptical. The story sounded too bizarre to be true. He left the men alone in the interview room but continued to listen to what they said. He was half expecting the men to start gloating about how their hoax was fooling the police, but instead Hickson and Parker continued to talk about their encounter in worried tones (see panel).

Now confident that the two men were telling him what they believed to be true, Sheriff Diamond arranged for them to have a medical examination at a nearby USAF base. The doctor found no signs of any injuries, nor of radiation, though both men did have a small cut similar to that used when taking blood samples.

A couple of days later, Parker had a nervous breakdown and was admitted to the hospital. Hickson, however, remained able to answer questions. He took a lie detector test, which he passed, and then underwent hypnotic regression to see if he could recall any further details about the encounter, but little more was revealed.

Alien Files

WERE PARKER AND HICKSON REALLY ABDUCTED?

The case appeared to be a dramatic and impressive account of abduction by aliens. However, later investigations found that the lie detector test had not been carried out according to standard procedure, so the results could not be relied upon. Moreover, the man who was on duty that night at a toll bridge just 270 m (900 ft) from the site of the encounter was questioned and said he had seen nothing all evening.

Some UFO researchers chose to reserve judgment on the case, but others accepted that Parker and Hickson really were victims of an alien abduction that evening. The two men later turned down a movie contract that would have brought them a considerable sum of money, saying that they just wanted to forget the whole affair.

The Day Encounter

On October 27, 1974, the Day family were driving home to Aveley in Essex, England. They were in a hurry to get back in time for a television program Mrs. Sue Day wanted to watch, which started at 9 PM. According to the Days, as they were driving they saw an oval blue light in the sky. The light seemed to follow them for a while, but then disappeared. A few minutes later, as the car rounded a bend, it was engulfed by a green mist. The car radio at once began buzzing with static, and John Day, fearing a short circuit, disconnected it. There was a bump as if the car had run over an object. Then they came out of the mist and drove home.

While John reconnected the car radio, Sue took the children indoors and put them to bed. Then she went back downstairs to watch her TV show. But the show was not on—the screen was filled with static. After fruitlessly trying to get a signal, she glanced at a clock and was astonished to see that it was almost midnight, at least two and a half hours later than it should have been. John could not explain the time lapse either.

Nightmares

In the weeks that followed, all the members of the family began to have strange dreams in which there was a recurrent image of a monstrous face. The children were particularly affected by the visions. Both John and Sue found themselves becoming increasingly interested in environmental issues, to which they had paid little attention before.

Eventually the nightmares got to be too much, and the Days consulted their doctor. He sent them to see Dr. Leonard Wilder, who studied trauma and sleep problems. Wilder thought that something may have happened during the missing time on October 27 that had inflicted trauma of some kind and that the Days had subconsciously blocked it from their minds to help them cope.

Wilder hypnotized both John and Sue to take them back in their memories to the night in question. The Days independently recalled almost identical tales. When the car had entered the green mist, the engine had first misfired and then died completely. Through the mist had then walked a group of aliens dressed in tight-fitting silver suits. These beings were over 1.8 m (6 ft) tall and generally human in appearance, except for the fact that they had catlike eyes of penetrating power.

The Day family had recurring nightmares of a sinister creature with catlike eyes.

These aliens escorted the Days from their car through the mist to the blue UFO and led them on board. Neither John nor Sue could recall any form of physical force being used. It was as if they had wanted to go with the aliens, perhaps in response to telepathic prompting of some kind.

Once inside the UFO the Days were handed over to a quite different group of aliens. These were about 1.2 m (4 ft) tall and dressed in white cloaks. They had animal-like faces with large eyes and pointed ears. It was these faces that had been haunting the dreams of the family. These creatures, the Days came to believe, were servants to the first group of aliens and had been trained by them to perform various duties. One of these was to conduct physical examinations of humans. The Days were then examined each in turn by the animal aliens.

Environmental Message

Once the medical tests were over, the taller aliens reappeared. They showed the family around the UFO, which was arranged on three decks. The aliens then told the Days that their home world was under threat of devastation by runaway pollution and other environmental threats of a less specific nature. They showed them a holographic film of their home planet and the threats it faced.

Although it was not specifically stated, the Days got the impression that the aliens had been visiting Earth to study humans for some considerable time. It also seemed that the aliens were carrying out tests or experiments that involved genetics or children in some way.

The Days then recalled being led back out of the blue UFO and through the green mist to their car. John started the engine and they set off. The moment they came out of the mist, their memories of the incident were wiped clean.

The Platner Encounter

Julio Platner was driving his van along a rural road near Winifreda, Argentina, on August 9, 1983. It was not yet dark when he claims he saw a bright, bluish light hovering over the road ahead of him. According to Platner's later testimony, he stopped the van and got out to try to get a better look at whatever the object was.

He was suddenly hit by a beam of brilliant light that dazzled him and sent him stumbling backward. He remembered falling, then came to, lying on a flat, hard table in a dimly lit room. The room was about 3 m (10 ft) across with curved walls that glowed slightly. Moving around him were four humanoid creatures. For some reason that he could not really explain, Platner thought that one of the aliens was a female. Platner tried to sit upright but was held firmly in place by one of the aliens gripping his shoulders. He tried to scream, but no sound came from his mouth.

One of the aliens came over to stare at Platner with its huge black eyes. Platner then received a telepathic message telling him not to worry as the aliens would not harm him. "What you are experiencing now," the Gray continued, "has happened to thousands of other people. When it is over you can talk of this if you like. Some people will believe you, but most will not."

After this communication, Platner became calmer and more relaxed. The female came over with a long, rigid tube that she filled with blood from Platner's arm. Further tests and medical examinations followed, lasting

about 20 minutes. Platner was told to stand up and was given his belongings. He then passed out once again. When he recovered consciousness, he was lying on top of the roof of his van about 1.6 km (1 mile) from where he had encountered the UFO. On his left arm was a small wound at the spot where the female Gray had extracted blood.

Alien Files

TYPICAL FEATURES OF ALIEN ABDUCTIONS

1. Missing time. Almost all witnesses discover, after encountering a UFO, that there is a period of time missing from their memory.

2. Nightmares. Commonly, witnesses experience nightmares, visions, or some kind of mental disturbance following the encounter.

3. Hypnotic regression. This leads witnesses to undergo hypnotic regression in order to find out what happened during the missing time.

4. Abduction. Hypnosis recovers apparent memories of being abducted, more or less unwillingly, by aliens.

5. Medical examination. Witnesses typically recall that, once inside the UFO, they were laid out on a table and subjected to physical examinations, which are frequently painful.

6. Departure. Witnesses are often given a tour of the UFO and then allowed to leave, retaining no memory of the experience.

Ageist Aliens

On August 12, 1983, Alfred Burtoo says he was sitting enjoying a quiet evening's fishing beside a canal in Berkshire, England, when he saw a light circling overhead. Assuming this to be a helicopter, Burtoo took little notice. He poured out a cup of tea from his flask as he watched the "helicopter" land a short distance away. Two short men left the object and began walking toward Burtoo, whose dog got up and began snarling. The figures were about 1.5 m (5 ft) tall and dressed in green overalls with headgear rather like motorcycle helmets with visors covering the face. The men asked Burtoo to accompany them. Burtoo put down his tea and followed them.

He climbed a short flight of steps into the UFO, having to duck his head as the doorway was very low. Once inside, Burtoo was bathed in an orange light for a few seconds. Then one of the figures asked him how old he was. Burtoo replied that he was 77. There was a hurried conversation between the two figures, after which one of them announced: "You can go now. You are too old and infirm for our purposes." Burtoo was hurriedly pushed out of the craft. The door was slammed shut behind him, and the UFO began to rise silently into the air as Burtoo went back to finish his cup of tea, which was now lukewarm.

What is Out There?

The sheer number of reports of alien encounters from different parts of the world, and the similarities between them, make the phenomenon hard to dismiss as nothing more than imaginary. Yet even if some of the stories are true, we don't know for sure that the creatures described in them are aliens. In fact, as skeptics point out, interstellar travel would take centuries, even at light speed, so the chances of visits from other habitable planets are actually pretty low. Other theories have been proposed, such as that they are visitors from another dimension, or can travel in time from Earth's future. Yet most scientists continue to believe that alien encounters are hallucinations. They point to the fact that alien appearances have changed over time according to fashion, from the beautiful "Nordics" of the 1950s and 1960s, to the more science-fiction "Grays" of today. Similar experiences were being described in the 19th century as encounters with

Alien Files

WHAT DID THE ALIENS LOOK LIKE?

The aliens, as described by Platner, appear to fit into the Gray category. The figures were basically human in shape, though their limbs and bodies were slender and rather elongated. They stood just over 1.2 m (4 ft) tall and were silvery-white. Platner was not certain if they were naked or dressed in very tight clothing. Their heads were entirely bald with domed foreheads. Their noses, mouths, and ears were tiny, but their eyes were huge and bulging without any eyelashes.

An alien Gray looms out of the mist. Many witnesses have reported being enveloped by a fog as the abduction takes place.

trolls or fairies. So is it just something about the human mind that sometimes causes us to think we have experienced something otherworldly? Or is there really something out there? We can only look at the evidence and decide for ourselves.

Chapter 4

Atlantis

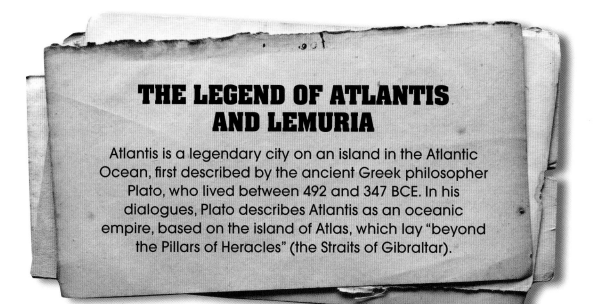

THE LEGEND OF ATLANTIS AND LEMURIA

Atlantis is a legendary city on an island in the Atlantic Ocean, first described by the ancient Greek philosopher Plato, who lived between 492 and 347 BCE. In his dialogues, Plato describes Atlantis as an oceanic empire, based on the island of Atlas, which lay "beyond the Pillars of Heracles" (the Straits of Gibraltar).

A Global Power

According to those people who believe in its reality, Atlantis existed in about 9,000 BCE (or the 1200s BCE, according to another interpretation). Its empire allegedly stretched from the North American copper mines of Michigan's Upper Peninsula, the shores of Mexico and Colombia in the west, to Italy and Egypt in the east, encompassing more territories and peoples than even the Roman Empire at its height. But, says Plato, in the middle of Atlantis's war against the Mediterranean world, the island of Atlas, of which Atlantis was the capital, sank "in a single day and night" of earthquakes and floods.

The Island and Its City

According to legend, the island of Atlas—named after a mythical Titan who supported the sky—was mountainous and broadly forested. South of its towering, dormant volcano was a plain 55 km (34 miles) long by 37 km (23 miles) wide. It was irrigated by a network of canals carrying water to the crops flourishing in the richly fertile volcanic soil.

South of this agricultural complex lay the city of Atlantis, capital of the oceanic empire. Plato records that the metropolis was made up of alternating circles of land and water, interconnected by bridged canals for both ship and foot traffic. Each of these artificial islands was surrounded by high walls interspersed with mighty watchtowers manned by soldiers. The smallest, central island bore the imperial residence and the magnificent Temple of Poseidon. A horse racetrack occupied the city's outermost land ring.

A visitor at that time, says Plato, would have been awed by the city's walls, not only for their enormous dimensions, but also for the sheets of orichalcum (high-grade copper) and mosaics of semi-precious minerals gleaming in the sunlight. The Temple of Poseidon was dominated, it is said, by a colossal statue of the sea god in his chariot, pulled by winged horses.

DID ATLANTIS EXIST?

The legend of Atlantis has been a source of fascination ever since it was rediscovered by scholars in the 17th century. But is there any truth to it? Atlantologists (seekers of Atlantis) speculate that a large landmass may once have existed in the location of the Mid-Atlantic Ridge. Geologists say that, if so, it would have been wracked by volcanoes and earthquakes, so it would have been an unlikely homeland. Most Plato scholars believe that his Atlantis was imaginary, or perhaps based on the island of Santorini in the Mediterranean, which was devastated by an eruption in about 1600 BCE. The arguments continue, and will probably only be settled when technological advances permit a systematic survey of the ocean floor.

The Temple of Poseidon stood in the middle, with a statue of the sea god as a charioteer overlooking the city.

cities and regions, but submitted to the judgment of the other rulers on any complaint made against them, as demanded by the laws of Poseidon. The laws also prevented the kings declaring making war on each other and required them to take united action against any external enemy.

Rulers of Atlantis

Plato explains that the empire was governed by ten kings, all directly descended from the sea-god founder of their empire. The kings had absolute power over their own

The head of the House of Atlas acted as emperor, whose decisions took precedent and were final. The laws of Poseidon encouraged the kings to rule with wisdom and restraint. Any who deviated from the laws were liable to charges of holy perjury and oath-breaking, and were subject to harsh punishments.

A Military Power

Legend tells us that at its height, Atlantis boasted immense armed forces to protect its far-flung empire. According to Plato, the Atlanteans fielded no fewer than 79,600 men-at-arms. These included 7,200 hoplites (heavily armed foot soldiers) and the same number of archers, supported by an additional 33,600 slingers and javelin-throwers. They were joined by 10,000 chariots, each one manned by a driver and warrior bearing a light shield. Atlantis was primarily a sea power. Her 14,400 naval personnel—marines, sailors, shipwrights, and dock hands—serviced 1,200 ships, which would have made it by far the biggest fleet of the ancient world.

Lemuria

Lemuria, or Mu, is the name of a mythical lost land said to have existed long ago in the Indian and/or Pacific Oceans. In 1864, zoologist Philip Sclater pointed out that fossils of lemurs and other related primates were found on Madagascar (an island off Africa) as well as in India. He proposed that both countries had once been part of a larger continent, which he named Lemuria (after "lemur"). Sclater's theory attracted support from some scientists, some of whom suggested that Lemuria had extended across parts of the Pacific Ocean as well.

Plato claimed that the citizens of Atlantis worshipped the sea god Poseidon.

Pacific Culture

The lost continent of Lemuria became a popular idea among 19th-century occultists such as Helena Blavatsky, William Scott-Elliot, and James Bramwell. According to their theories, Mu was a culture that spread its influence over many Pacific islands before they were swallowed up by the ocean. Forced to abandon their homes, the Lemurians dispersed, settling in Melanesia and Polynesia. Some moved to the Americas, influencing the early cultures there. By studying and comparing modern-day Pacific cultures, the occultists tried to construct a picture of what they believed to be a single root culture: Lemuria.

The occultists suggested that Mu existed at the same time as Atlantis, but the two places were very different. While Atlantis was a technologically advanced, imperialist culture, the Lemurians were a simple, devout, seafaring people whose chief purpose in sailing to other parts of the world was to spread their spiritual beliefs.

Architecture

The Lemurians made ceremonial buildings, sacred sculptures, and roads, but no cities. The evidence for this, according to the occultists, lay in Mu's influence on later cultures—for example, the roads in Micronesia's Tonga and Malden Island, the monumental sculpted heads of Mexico's Olmecs, the colossi of Easter Island, and the ancient city at Nan Madol in the Caroline Islands. Based on this evidence, the occultists believe that Lemurian building styles were largely right-angled and rectangular, contrasting with Atlantean architecture, which was predominantly curved and circular.

LOST WORLD FILES

DID LEMURIA EXIST?

The scientific community no longer believes that Lemuria existed—at least not in the Indian Ocean. According to the theory of plate tectonics, accepted now by all geologists, Madagascar and India were indeed once part of the same landmass, but plate movement caused India to break away millions of years ago and move to its present location. The original landmass broke apart—it did not sink beneath the sea.

Music, Art and Language

According to believers in Lemuria, the Lemurians were a musically skilled people, excelling in the performance of a cappella singing, yet another legacy preserved among the Polynesians. They created sand-paintings, an art that spread with their migrations to the American Southwest, among the Navaho Indians, and, in the opposite direction, to Asia.

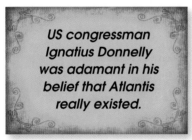

US congressman Ignatius Donnelly was adamant in his belief that Atlantis really existed.

an additional 26 overseas editions. The book is still published in more than a dozen languages and remains a core textbook of Atlantology.

Rudolf Steiner (1861–1925), founder of the Steiner educational movement, was highly influential in the growing field of Atlantology. His 1904 work *Cosmic Memory: Prehistory of Earth and Man* maintained that the Atlanteans formed one of humankind's "root races," a people who did not require speech, but communicated telepathically in images. According to Steiner, the story of Atlantis can be found repeated in Germanic myth. Steiner wrote that the Atlanteans were the first people to develop the concept of good versus evil, and laid the groundwork for all ethical and legal systems.

The work of promoting Atlantis was later taken up by the Austrian physicist Otto Heinrich Muck (1883–1965). In his book *The Secret of Atlantis* (1965) he attempted to offer a scientific evaluation of Plato's account of Atlantis. Charles Berlitz (1913–2003) also helped revive popular interest in the subject with his books *The Mystery of Atlantis* (1974) and *Atlantis, the Eighth Continent* (1984). A talented linguist, Berlitz concluded that many modern and ancient languages derive from a single prehistoric source, which he traced to Atlantis.

Atlantean Scholarship

The man most responsible for bringing Atlantis to the attention of the wider public was Ignatius Donnelly (1831–1901), a US congressman and founder of Atlantology. Donnelly's 1882 book *Atlantis, the Antediluvian World* was a runaway bestseller. Within a few years of its release, it had sold out 23 American editions and

The Destruction of Atlantis

The French astronomer G.R. Corli (1744–1806) was the first person to suggest that Atlantis was destroyed by an extraterrestrial impact. In 1785 he put forward the idea that a fragment from a passing comet collided with the Earth, causing a cataclysm that wiped out the legendary island. Nearly 100 years later, Ignatius Donnelly, in his book, *Ragnarok: Age of Fire and Gravel* (1884), also proposed that the island had been annihilated by a comet's collision with the Earth.

Atlantis—Comets and Asteroids

In the 1920s and 1930s, Donnelly's theory was revived and supported by the German physicist Hans Hoerbiger (1860–1931), who believed that the Atlantean catastrophe could have occurred as the result of the Earth's impact with a cometary fragment of frozen debris. Immanuel Velikovsky (1895–1979), in *Worlds in Collision* (1950), elaborated on the possibility of a celestial impact as responsible for the sudden extinction of a pre-flood empire. Intriguing as these theories were, they were largely unsupported by physical evidence. But many Atlantologists believed physical evidence was found in 1964 when a German researcher, Otto Muck, announced his discovery of twin deep-sea holes in the ocean floor. According to Muck, they were caused by a small asteroid that split in half and set off a chain reaction of geological violence along the length of the Mid-Atlantic Ridge, a line of subsurface volcanoes to which the island of Atlantis was supposedly connected.

In the late 1980s and early 1990s, astronomers Victor Clube and Bill Napier put forward their "fire from heaven" theory to explain the destruction of Atlantis. According to them, the destruction came about not through a single collision but a bombardment of dozens or hundreds of small meteorites as our planet passed through or near a large cloud of debris from the disintegration of a giant comet.

LEGENDARY TALES

THE PLEIADES

In North America, the Cherokee Indians remembered Unadatsug, a group of stars—the Pleiades—one of which "creating a fiery tail, fell to Earth. Where it landed a palm tree grew up, and the fallen star transformed into an old man, who warned of coming floods." Similar accounts may be found among the Quiche Maya of the Lowland Yucatán, the Muysica of Colombia, the Arawak Indians of Venezuela, the Aztecs at Cholula, the ancient Greeks, and in Jewish scriptures. According to the Jewish Talmud: "When the Holy One, blessed be He, wished to bring the Deluge upon the world, He took two stars out of the Pleiades."

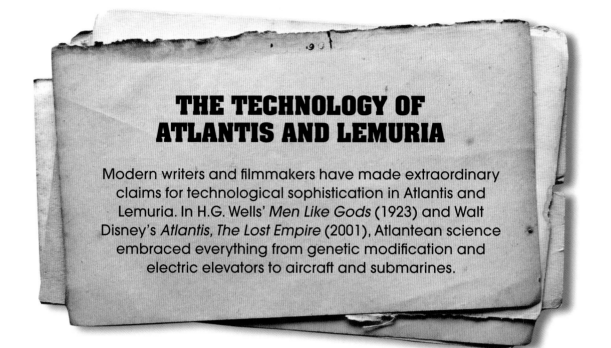

THE TECHNOLOGY OF ATLANTIS AND LEMURIA

Modern writers and filmmakers have made extraordinary claims for technological sophistication in Atlantis and Lemuria. In H.G. Wells' *Men Like Gods* (1923) and Walt Disney's *Atlantis, The Lost Empire* (2001), Atlantean science embraced everything from genetic modification and electric elevators to aircraft and submarines.

Lost Science

Atlantologists believe they have uncovered fascinating clues of a kind of "superscience" existing in deep antiquity. However most scientists and historians reject the idea of a technologically advanced, prehistoric race, mainly because there is no

Is it possible that peoples of the distant past could have had access to advanced technology?

archaeological evidence for this.

Atlantologists dispute the idea that a graph of human technological progress over time would show a constantly ascending line. They argue that there are many examples of ancient cultures creating technologies that were then forgotten when their societies collapsed, only to be rediscovered hundreds of years later. However much of the ancient "technology" that they cite as evidence of this theory, many scientists argue, is also legendary. For example, Atlantologists purport that Mayan understanding of celestial mechanics was not matched until the late 20th century. They also argue that ancient Inca agricultural techniques yielded three times as much produce as farming methods employed in today's Peru.

When the story of Atlantis was being written by Plato in the fourth century BCE, some of his fellow Greeks were sailing in the *Alexandris*, a colossal ship supposedly more than 120 m (440 ft) in length, the dimensions of which would not be seen again for another 2,000 years. Another classic example of Atlantologists is a pregnancy test allegedly performed by 18th-Dynasty Egyptians, which was not rediscovered until the 1920s. However, regardless of the dubious veracity of some of these claims, it is nonetheless true that many other skills and technologies have been lost with the fall of past nations, only to be rediscovered many centuries later.

LOST WORLD FILES

THE BAGHDAD BATTERY

In 1938, German archaeologist Dr. Wilhelm Koenig was making an inventory of artifacts at the Iraq State Museum in Baghdad when he became intrigued by a collection of 2,000-year-old clay jars. Each of the jars contained a copper cylinder capped at the bottom by a copper disk and sealed with asphalt. Koenig was struck by their resemblance to a series of modern, dry-cell storage batteries. After the Second World War, Willard Gray, a technician at the General Electric High Voltage Laboratory in Pittsfield, Massachusetts, built an exact reproduction of the Baghdad jars. He found that, when filled with citric acid, an iron rod inserted into the copper tube generated 1.5 to 2.75 volts of electricity. It was not much, but sufficient to, for example, electroplate an object with gold. His experiment demonstrated that practical electricity might possibly have been applied to metalworking by ancient craftsmen.

Atlantologists speculate that the "Baghdad Battery" was probably not the first of its kind, but offered a glimpse of a hitherto unsuspected ancient technology – a technology that may have included far more impressive feats of electrical engineering long since lost.

Ancient Aviators

The first documented aerial voyages took place even before Plato was born, when a fifth-century BCE scientist, Archytas of Tarentum, invented a leather kite large enough to carry a young boy. In the earliest known example of aerial reconnaissance, the high-flying young man actually served as an observer for Greek armies on campaign.

Atlantologists conjecture that the technology of flight may have been mastered even further back in history. In 1898 a model was found in an Egyptian tomb near Sakkara in the Upper Nile Valley.

It was called "bird" and catalogued Object 6347 at the Egyptian Museum in Cairo. Dr. Khalil Massiha, examining the artifact in 1969, was startled to see that the "bird" not only had straight wings but also an upright tailfin. To Dr. Massiha, the object appeared to be that of a model plane. It is made of wood, weighs 39.12 g (1.38 oz) and remains in good condition. The "aircraft's" length and wingspan are both 18 cm (7 in) and its nose is 3.2 cm (1.25 in) long. The extremities of the object and the wingtips are aerodynamically shaped. Apart from a symbolic eye and two short lines under the wings, it has no decorations, nor has it any landing legs.

In all, 14 similar flying models have been recovered from ancient digs in Egypt, dating from the Roman era back to the start of the Old Kingdom in the early third millennium BCE. The Sakkara specimen, for example, was retrieved from an archaeological zone identified with the earliest dynastic periods, at the very beginning of Egyptian expansion. This suggests that the model was not a later development, but belonged to the first years of settlement in the Nile Valley. Could these artifacts have been models of real flying machines, operated by the Egyptians' Atlantean forefathers? Many Atlantologists believe so.

Vimana and Pauwvotas

There are references in the scriptures of ancient India to so-called Vimana aircraft, supposedly flown in ancient times. These appear in the epics Ramayana,

Mahabharata and Drona Parva. Other classic sources, namely the Vimaanika Shastra, Manusa, and Samarangana Sutradhara, describe "aerial cars," which, they allege, were operating in prehistoric times.

Similarly, Hopi Indians of the North American southwest told of *pauwvotas*—airborne vehicles flown over immense distances by an ancestral people, before their beautiful island perished during a Great Deluge.

However, these alleged machines would have had little in common with modern aviation—there's no hint of how they were powered, since there are no references in the stories to anything resembling propellers, jet engines, or other essential elements of aeronautics.

Atlantologists think that these folk memories of Vimanas, *pauwvotas,* and the Orichana are all that remain of a lost Atlantean supertechnology that once, millennia before the Wright brothers, created some kind of aircraft.

Could the flying temples of the Hindu scriptures have been inspired by real Atlantean technology?

85

Building

Atlantologists believe that the Atlanteans excelled in the area of building, and that they may have spread those skills around the world. Could the ancient Egyptians have learned their building skills from Atlanteans? The Egyptians record that Thaut, survivor of the flood that brought his fellow "Followers of Horus" to the Nile Delta at the dawn of Egyptian settlement, was the Great Pyramid's chief architect.

Mining

The Menemonie Indians of North America's Upper Great Lakes region tell of the "Marine Men"—white-skinned people from across the Atlantic Ocean, who blasphemed against Mother Earth by "digging out her shiny bones." Atlantologists believe that this is a reference to copper miners who excavated more than half a billion tonnes (551,155,655 tons) of the raw metal between 3100 and 1200 BCE. The miners were apparently able to determine the precise location of underground veins by dropping "magical stones"—known to the Menomonie as *yuwipi*—which made the copper-bearing rock "ring, as brass does." Could the pale-faced foreigners have been Atlanteans using their mining skills in North America?

This account from the Menemonie recalls a prospecting technique used by ancient European miners more than 3,000 years ago. Bronze with a high tin content—from one part in four to one in six or seven—emits a full, resonant sound when struck with a stone. Such bronze is today known as "bell metal" for the ringing tone it produces.

Lemuria's "Wonder of the World"

According to the occultists who believe in the existence of Lemuria, that lost world had a more spiritual character than the materialistic Atlantis, and was less inclined toward technological innovation. Nevertheless, the occultists claim that Lemuria was responsible for the largest food factory ever constructed and one of humankind's greatest feats of engineering.

Today it is described as the "Eighth Wonder of the World"

Seeker's Account

PLATO DESCRIBES THE WALLS OF ATLANTIS

"The entire circuit of the wall which went around the outermost one they covered with a coating of brass, and the circuit of the next wall they coated with tin, and the third, which encompassed the citadel, flashed with the red light of orichalcum (high-grade copper)."

The extraordinary Banaue rice terraces have been described as the "Eighth Wonder of the World."

and it still exists at Luzon in the Philippines, 250 km (156 miles) north of Manila. A tremendous stairway rises to 915 m (3,000 ft) above the valley floor, forming an ascending series of artificial plateaus for the growing of rice. From bottom to top, the stairway exceeds the height of the world's tallest skyscraper. The Banaue rice terraces, as they are known, cover more than 10,360 sq km (4,000 sq miles) of the Cordillera mountain range. If laid end to end, their paddies would form a line stretching halfway around the Earth. Even so, occultists believe that less than 50 percent of the original agricultural network survives. They say that when they were functioning at their maximum capacity more than 2,000 years ago, the Banaue rice terraces yielded prodigious quantities of crops. This was not only due to their vast scale, but because of their highly efficient irrigation system fed by water from the rainforests above the terraces.

The occultists suggest that the Banaue rice terraces could have yielded enough food to feed several million people, and they imply the existence of a highly developed Pacific society during prehistory, currently unknown to archaeology.

THE SEARCH FOR ATLANTIS

In March 2003, American psychologist Dr. Gregory Little and his wife, Lora, were trying to verify a strange sighting made eleven years earlier. They had been told of a wall-like structure lurking below 1 m (3.3 ft) of water in the Atlantic Ocean. The sunken enigma was said to lie near Andros Island, 240 km (150 miles) southeast of Miami, Florida. Andros is the largest island of the Bahamas, and also the greatest tract of unexplored land in the Western Hemisphere, thanks to its profuse, often impenetrable mangrove swamps.

The Littles were following up on the claims of a local dive operator, Dino Keller. In 1992 he claimed to have sailed over a shallow coral reef, where he observed the underwater "wall." His description of the object as a "wall" was puzzling because archaeologists believe that Andros remained uninhabited until the 17th century.

What long-forgotten secrets could be hidden beneath the waters of the Atlantic Ocean?

Andros Platform

Following Keller's directions, the Littles swam about 600 m (1,968 ft) from shore to find a 458-m (1,503-ft) long, 50-m (164-ft) wide arrangement of massive blocks in three, well-ordered sloping tiers, interspersed by two bands of smaller stones. Although standing 3 m (10 ft) beneath the surface, its top section was more than 1 m (3.3 ft) deep, just as described by Keller. The Littles also found a ramp leading from the floor of the lagoon to the top of the platform.

The feature's regular appearance and almost uniformly square-cut blocks suggested to the Littles that it was made by humans. Given its location at a natural bay in the North Atlantic Current, they thought it may have been a quay, breakwater, or port facility of some kind.

The structure contained a number of rectangular holes 13 cm (5 in) wide and deep. The Littles speculated that these may have held mooring pylons used to tie up docked ships. Some investigators who have since studied the blocks have suggested they may have been quarried from local beach rock and deliberately set in place, a marine construction practice that was common throughout the ancient world.

But who could have built such a massive project at a time when territory now covered by the ocean was dry land? And were the Andros Platform and Joulter Cays wall the only structures of their kind in the vicinity or merely part of a much larger complex yet to be found?

Precise dating of the sunken structures is problematical, but Dr. Little believes the two structures are stylistically related and he estimates that the Andros Platform dates prior to 10,000 BCE. Sea levels were low enough then for its creation on dry land. Atlantologists point out that the Andros Platform has six alternating bands of stone. Six was the sacred numeral of Atlantis, whose city planners, according to Plato, incorporated the holy number in the capital's alternating stone walls.

An Atlantean Outpost?

Despite the dramatic discoveries off Andros, Atlantologists believe that the western Atlantic is an unlikely location for the lost capital. Plato described the island of Atlas as mountainous, fertile, seismically unstable, populated by elephants, and geographically situated to invade the Mediterranean World. None of these characteristics apply to the Bahamas. These formations are, in the opinion of most Atlantologists, more likely to be the remains of a western outpost of the Atlantean empire. Nevertheless, Atlantologists are extremely excited by the discoveries. If they are not exactly Atlantis, they say, they may nonetheless be the first example of Atlantean remains found since its disappearance. For Atlantis itself, say Atlantologists, researchers would be better off looking elsewhere, beneath the waves of the northeast Atlantic.

THE SEARCH FOR LEMURIA

In 1985, a Japanese scuba instructor was diving in the waters off Yonaguni, among the Ryukyu chain of islands. As he glided through the depths some 13 m (43 ft) beneath the clear, blue Pacific, the diver was suddenly confronted by what appeared to be a great stone building heavily encrusted with coral.

Yonaguni's Drowned Enigma

Coming closer, he observed that the colossal structure was an arrangement of monolithic blocks. After circling the formation several times and photographing it with his underwater camera, he rose to the surface, reoriented himself, and kicked to shore. Next day, the photographs he took appeared in Japan's leading newspapers.

The structure sparked controversy and drew crowds of diving archaeologists, media people, and curious amateurs, none of whom was able to ascertain its identity. They could not even agree if it was human-made, let alone ancient or modern. Was it the remnant of some forgotten coastal

This artist's rendering shows the sunken monument lying in the waters off the Japanese island of Yonaguni.

defensive installation from the war, or could it be something entirely different and far older? Already there were whispers of the lost culture of Mu, preserved in legend as the vanished motherland of humankind, which subsided beneath the waves long before the beginning of recorded time. Sceptics did not believe it was human-made at all, but an entirely natural formation. It was hard to prove one way or the other, as the enigma was sealed within a thick encrustation of coral.

Arch or Gateway?

Then, in late summer of the following year, another diver exploring the waters around Yonaguni was shocked to behold what seemed to be a massive arch or gateway of huge stone blocks. The rocks seemed well fitted together in a manner compared by some to prehistoric masonry found among Inca cities on the other side of the Pacific. In this case, thanks to the swift currents in the area, coral had been unable to gain any foothold on the structure, leaving it unobscured in the 30-m (98-ft) visibility of the crystal-clear waters. Many were convinced it was human-made and extremely old.

Could this arch or gateway be evidence of a lost culture? Many Lemuria-seekers think so. They point out that the ancient city of Tiahuanaco in the Bolivian Andes, for example, contains two ceremonial gates. Sacred gates also appear on the Polynesian island of Tonga and on Japan.

LOST WORLD FILES

WARTIME INVESTIGATION

Forty years before the discoveries off Yonaguni, during the Second World War, US Navy divers made an intriguing find in the same area. In the course of their extensive preparations to invade the island of Okinawa (the largest of the Ryuku Islands) in 1945, US Navy planners issued detailed maps to the commanders of their landing craft, showing the optimum areas for quickly and safely disembarking their troops. During the invasion, several warships approached the coast to provide support for the landing craft and engage enemy shore batteries. Instead of the open water they expected to find, they scraped their keels along underwater obstructions not included on the maps provided by the navy planners.

After the battle, divers went over the side to investigate. The so-called "hard-hat divers," who wore copper helmets pumped with air supplied by their shipmates above, expected to find a secret enemy installation. Instead, they were surprised to see what appeared to be a massive stone platform with broad steps. The divers' brief report, made around the time of the Japanese surrender, did not describe the discovery as a modern structure. They said it appeared to be the remains of an ancient stone building. Their report may still be somewhere in the US military archives, but whatever impact it might have made at the time was utterly eclipsed by the Allies' euphoria on VJ Day.

Spiral Staircase

In spring, 1998, divers encountered another mysterious formation 1,125 km (703 miles) from Okinawa. The find is located near the uninhabited islet of Okinoshima in the Korean Strait, 45 km (28 miles) off the mainland at Kyushu.

One of the divers, Shun-Ichiroh Moriyama, observed what appeared to be a row of huge pillars standing more than 30 m (98 ft) beneath the surface, about 400 m (1,312 ft) off the northeastern shore of Okinoshima. He counted four of them, each one an enormous 7–10 m (23–33 ft) across and almost 30 m (98 ft) tall. On closer inspection, divers could see that they resembled not pillars but round stone towers, one of which appeared to have a spiral staircase winding around its exterior. For some, this tower called to mind an Australian Aboriginal folk tale of a drowned "Land of Perfection," with a great "crystal cone" tower entwined with a spiral "snake."

News of this discovery made the front pages of Japan's major newspapers, and prompted the making of a television documentary

The underwater blocks appeared to be a staircase curling around the outside of a tower.

about the find, including underwater video coverage of the peculiar structures. Even in the clear waters of the Korean Strait they were not easily photographed, however, owing to their great size. Subsurface visibility of more than 30 m (98 ft) is needed to see the monuments in their entirety, but around Okinosha, visibility extends no further than 13–16 m (43–52 ft). But the grand "staircase" that spirals around the lower farthest to the east was photographed. Divers from the university at Fukuoka measured its steps and found them to be uniformly cut to a depth of 40 cm (16 in), with a width varying from 150–180 cm (59–71 in).

Oceanographic Research

Despite an abundance of Pacific islander folk traditions describing a sunken homeland, the first accurate sonar-generated maps of the ocean bottom reveal nothing resembling a lost continent. The charts do nonetheless show areas of the Pacific that were dry land until relatively recently.

The Archipel des Tuamotu is a large collection of shallow features running northwest to southeast about 33 km (21 miles) northeast of Tahiti. Other formerly above-water areas include the Emperor Seamount Chain, extending from north to south in the western Pacific, the Caroline Seamounts, and the Shatsky Rise. Taken together, these suggest a prehistoric Pacific containing rather more dry land than was previously imagined.

The chart also shows a sometimes very shallow and long, relatively thin ridge of subsurface islands running in a chain from the southern tip of Japan, including the Ryukyu chain, where the sunken monuments were found at Okinawa, Yonaguni, and other islands. Lemuria-seekers concede that this is not evidence of a sunken continent. Nonetheless,

they contend, these once-dry lands comprised large territories over which a Lemurian settlement may once have spread across part of the Pacific Ocean.

OTHER LOST WORLDS

Atlantis and Lemuria may be humankind's most famous lost cultures, but there are other phantom realms that play powerful roles in the mythology of different peoples. The lure of these fabled worlds, and the riches they may contain, have tempted many explorers to try and find them.

The Seven Cities of Gold

Invading Spaniards in the early 16th century observed Colombia's Chibchan Indians carrying out the so-called Guatavita ceremony in commemoration of their forefather, a legendary golden king. The Spanish convinced themselves the king's city, "El Dorado," still existed somewhere in the Colombian interior, and they spent several fruitless centuries searching for it.

While the conquistadors were searching for El Dorado across Colombia, their comrades in North America marched after the legendary Seven Cities of Gold. The cities were sometimes collectively referred to as Quivira or Cíbola, and their story predated the Spanish Conquest by 350 years. It began in 1150 CE, when seven bishops and their congregations fled Spain by ship, carrying away certain religious relics, before the Moors could seize the city of Mérida.

This is a Colombian ceremonial gold mask. European explorers became convinced that the city of El Dorado contained countless such treasures.

The refugees were never heard from again, and it was said that they had crossed the Atlantic Ocean to land on another continent, where they set up seven cities, one for each bishop, soon growing rich in gold and precious stones. The legend persisted over the centuries, but its popularity swelled following the Spanish conquest of Mexico.

Place of the Seven Caves

In 1519, the Aztec emperor Moctezuma II told the leader of the Spanish conquistadors, Hernán Cortés, that the Aztecs had previously lived to the north of their current capital, Tenochtitlan, in a place called Chicomoztoc. Hearing its translation as the "Place of the Seven Caves," the Spanish concluded that the Aztecs' former residence was none other than the fabled Cíbola. In reality, Chicomoztoc was either Rock Lake in distant Wisconsin or a large if humble settlement built around a height near the present-day town of San Isidro Culhuacan, 100 km (63 miles) northeast of the Valley of Mexico. Neither place contained any gold.

Spurred on by inflated claims for Chicomoztoc and other local tales describing far-off cities overflowing with riches, Viceroy Antonio de Mendoza dispatched an expedition led by Marcos de Niza, a Franciscan monk, in search of Cíbola. After ten months, de Niza returned to claim that he had visited a busy place whose residents ate from dishes of gold and silver, decorated their houses with turquoise, and adorned themselves with enormous pearls, emeralds, and other stunning gems.

Certain that the Seven Cities of Gold were there for the taking, de Mendoza ordered their conquest. The expedition was led by Francisco Vásquez de Coronado, who set out from Culiacán at the head of the viceroy's well-equipped army on April 22, 1540. But by the time he reached the Arizona desert, Coronado knew that de Niza had lied.

LEGENDARY TALES

MOUNTAIN RANGE OF SILVER

In South America, Spanish invaders were lured into the interior with hopes of finding Sierra de la Plata, the "Mountain Range of Silver." Survivors of an early-16th-century shipwreck on the Argentine coast had received abundant gifts of silver from the natives, who spoke of several mountains rich in the metal. Soon afterward the Spaniards discovered the estuary of the Uruguay and Paraná Rivers, which they called the Río de la Plata, the "River of Silver," known in English as the Plate River, because they believed it led to Sierra del Plata. Although the Río de la Plata became a prosperous mining area, the Mountain Range of Silver was never found. Nevertheless, as a demonstration of the power of myth, Argentina derived its name from the Latin word for "silver," *argentum*.

City of the Caesars

A myth arose that ancient Roman sailors, fleeing civil unrest following Julius Caesar's assassination, were shipwrecked on the Straits of Magellan at the southern tip of South America. For many decades following the discovery of the New World, stories spread of El Ciudad de los Césares, the "City of the Caesars," also known as the "City of the Patagonia." The city was said to be awash with gold, silver, and diamonds given by grateful Incas in gratitude for Roman help in building them an extensive network of roads.

The City of the Caesars was never found, but some intriguing discoveries have been made that suggest the Romans may well have reached South America. For example, a Roman shipwreck was investigated by underwater archaeologist Robert Marx, off Rio de Janeiro, in 1976. Amphorae he retrieved from the vessel were studied by Elizabeth Will, a professor in Classical Greek history at the University of Massachusetts. She positively identified them as part of a cargo from the Mediterranean port of Zilis, dating to around 250 CE. Marx went on to find a bronze fibula—a garment clasp—in Brazil's Guanabarra Bay.

Further north, near the Mexican Gulf Coast, bricks used to build the Mayan city of Comalcalco were found to be stamped with second-century CE Roman mason marks, while its terracotta plumbing—unique in all Mesoamerica—was identical to contemporary pipes found in Israel. These

and similar finds—such as the ceramic representation of a bearded European with a Roman-style haircut and wearing a typically Roman cap, retrieved during the excavation of a second-century CE pyramid at Caliztlahuaca, Mexico—suggest that the legend of the "City of the Caesars" may have some basis in truth.

Antilia

Antilia is a legendary island that was reputed to lie in the Atlantic Ocean, far to the west of Portugal and Spain. The earliest known description of Antilia appeared in a biography of the Roman military commander Quintus Sertorius, written by the historian Plutarch in 74 CE. According to Plutarch, in about 83 BCE, during Sertorius's consulship in Spain, he "met some sailors who had recently come back from the Atlantic islands, two in number separated by a very narrow strait and lie 10,000 furlongs from Africa." The sailors described Antilia as a utopian realm with fertile soil and a fine climate, producing plenty of food for its happy people.

Antilia was more or less forgotten until the 15th century when voyages of discovery into the Atlantic Ocean rekindled interest in the island. In a Portuguese version of the Spanish Cíbola myth, it was said that seven Portuguese bishops and their parishioners rediscovered Antilia after fleeing from the Moorish conquest of Iberia. After their arrival on the island, they supposedly founded the cities of Aira, Anhuib, Ansalli, Ansesseli, Ansodi, Ansolli, and Con. Nuremberg geographer Martin Behaim repeated the legend on his 1492 globe of the Earth. An inscription on the globe stated that the crew of a Spanish vessel sighted Antilia in 1414 and Portuguese sailors landed there during the 1430s. Antilia had been included in European maps from as early as 1424, and the renowned mathematician Paul Toscanelli advised Christopher Columbus before his 1492 voyage that Antilia was the principal landmark for measuring the distance between Lisbon and Zipangu (Japan).

The island of Antilia was usually depicted as an almost perfect rectangle, its long axis running north–south, but with seven or eight bays between the east and west coasts. This shape bears a vague resemblance to Puerto Rico, which led some geographers to believe that Puerto Rico was indeed Plutarch's Antilia. As a consequence, the Caribbean islands became known as the Antilles.

Antilia in the Azores?

Antilia has also been identified by some as San Miguel, the largest island in the Azores. San Miguel matches Plutarch's description in terms of distance from Morocco—1,825 km (1,141 miles)—but its shape and size does not match its representation on Renaissance maps. Antilia was usually shown about the size of Portugal, which is 92,090 sq km (35,645 sq miles), but San Miguel is just 744.5 sq km (287 sq miles).

The Azores were uninhabited at the time of their discovery in 1427, but the the Portugese sailors who first landed there found evidence of previous visitors from Europe. Inside a cave on Santa Maria, the Portuguese stumbled upon a stone altar adorned with serpentine designs. At Corvo, a small cask of Phoenician coins dating to the fifth century BCE was found.

A more dramatic find was a bronze statue on top of a mountain on San Miguel itself. It was 5 m (16 ft) tall with a stone pedestal bearing a badly weathered inscription. On top of a magnificently crafted

Could San Miguel in the Azores be the real Antilia?

THE DRAGON'S ISLE

Fifteenth-century Arab geographers referred to Antilia as Jezirat al Tennyn, the "Dragon's Isle," evoking an island of active volcanoes, a description that hardly fits Puerto Rico. San Miguel, however, boasts numerous volcanoes, one of which, interestingly, is known as Sete Cidades, the "Seven Cities." Its crater is about 53 miles (5 km) across, with walls some 1,640 ft (500 m) high. Sete Cidades has erupted at least eight times since 1444; another of the island's volcanoes, Agua de Pau, erupted for almost a month in 1563; an unnamed group of volcanoes erupted in 1652; and, just offshore, the Monaco Bank submarine volcano blew up in 1907, and again four years later. But San Miguel's largest, most dangerous volcano is Furnas. With a summit caldera about 3.75 miles (6 km) in diameter and 984 to 1,312 ft (300 to 400 m) deep, Furnas generated a week-long eruption in 1630, which claimed the lives of more than 200 people, mostly in swift, boiling mud flows. With this record, San Miguel certainly matches Arabic descriptions of Antilia as the "Dragon's Isle."

horse sat the rider with his right arm stretched forward to point across the sea toward the west. When notified of the discovery, King John V ordered it removed to Portugal, but the statue slipped from its improvised halter and crashed down the side of the mountain. The rider's head, one arm, and the horse's head and flank were the only parts to survive the fall. These fragments, together with an impression of the pedestal's inscription, were sent to the king.

They were preserved in his royal palace in Lisbon, where scholars were baffled by what they described as the inscription's "archaic Latin." They could only decipher one word from it—cates—but its meaning eluded them. Atlantologists point out that the word is close to *cati*, which means "go that way" in Quechua, the language spoken by the Incas. Unfortunately, modern scholars have been denied the chance of further investigation of the statue and inscription: in 1755, all the artifacts removed from San Miguel were lost during the great earthquake that destroyed most of Lisbon.

Chapter 5

Bigfoot

BIGFOOT: FIRST IMPRESSIONS

The native peoples of North America are the source of the oldest stories about Bigfoot, or Sasquatch. Each tribe had its own name for it. They called it *wendigo, chenoo,* or *kiwakwe.* They all described a creature covered in fur that looked like a very large human and lived in remote forested areas. As early as 1793, European settlers in North America were reporting sightings of a "hairy ape-man." A legend soon grew up of a "wild man of the woods," and there were several newspaper reports of scary encounters by hunters and trappers during the 19th and early 20th centuries.

The Battle of Ape Canyon

Then, in 1924, the *Oregonian* newspaper from Portland, Oregon, carried a story that was unlike the others. The report related the account of five gold prospectors who had been panning for gold around the Lewis River, close to Mount St. Helens. The prospectors—Fred Beck, Marion Smith, Roy Smith, Gabe Lafever, and John Peterson—had been working their claim for over two years by the time of the alleged encounter.

According to the men, one afternoon in July 1924, they began to hear a noise as if somebody was banging loudly on a hollow wooden trunk. This was followed by a loud whistling call coming from a

APE-MAN FILE

CRYPTIDS

A cryptid is a creature whose existence is claimed in stories or legends, but which is not acknowledged by science. Bigfoot, and the other creatures described in this chapter, are all apelike cryptids. Do they exist? Scientists argue that eyewitness reports, however numerous or credible, are not sufficient evidence to prove a creature exists. They point to the fact that witnesses might mistake a sighting of one creature for something else, or be the victims of hoaxes. What is needed is hard evidence, such as a body, that can be independently studied and verified.

wooded ridge that overlooked their camp. After a week of this, the men habitually carried their rifles with them when collecting firewood or water.

One day, Marion Smith and Fred Beck were fetching water when—so they later claimed—they saw one of the "mountain gorillas" about 91 m (300 ft) away. It stood about 2.13 m (7 ft) tall on its hind legs, and it was watching the two men from behind a pine tree. Smith fired three shots but only hit the tree, so the creature ran off uninjured. When it reappeared from the trees, now about 183 m (600 ft) away, Beck fired but missed. They ran back to the cabin to consult with the others. Faced by gigantic, man-like creatures, the prospectors decided to depart. However, it was getting late in the day, so they decided to stay the night rather than risk being caught in the woods in the dark with the "mountain gorillas."

Could the forests around Mount St. Helens be home to the Sasquatch?

Midnight Attack

At midnight, the men later alleged, they were awoken by a terrific thump as something hit the cabin wall. The sound of heavy footfalls came from outside the cabin, and Smith peered out through a chink between the logs to see three of the huge creatures. It also sounded as if there were others nearby. The creatures then picked up large rocks with which they began to pound at the walls. The men grabbed their guns and prepared to face the beasts if they should break in.

According to the men, at least two of the apes got onto the roof and began jumping up and down. Another began pounding on the door, which Beck braced shut with a wooden pole. After several terrifying minutes, the assault ended and the creatures slipped away into the darkness. But less than an hour later they were back. Again they attacked the cabin, trying to break in, and again they retreated, only to return with redoubled fury to the assault.

Yowie

Orang Pendek
Pendak

Yeren

Yeti

Maricoxi

Wildman

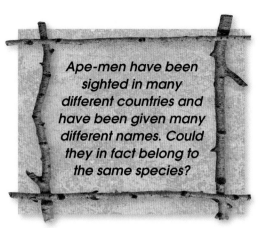

Ape-men have been sighted in many different countries and have been given many different names. Could they in fact belong to the same species?

to find the cabin. Although some days had passed, the signs of the assault were still to be seen and the cabin was surrounded by gigantic footprints—some of which were ominously fresh. The reporters, like the miners, got out quickly. The place was dubbed Ape Canyon by the press, and it is known by that name to this day.

Ostman's Encounter

Soon after the newspapers carried the story of the Battle of Ape Canyon, stories spread through the area that a young man named Albert Ostman had been kidnapped by the "mountain gorillas" and that he had lived with his captors for some time.

In the summer of 1924, Ostman was working in British Columbia. He decided to take a break and went up into the mountains to look for gold. When he returned to camp one night, he noticed that his things had been disturbed. Blaming animals looking for food, Ostman decided to tuck his rifle into his sleeping bag.

According to Ostman, he awoke when he found himself being picked up in his

Finally, as dawn broke, the creatures left. After a while, the terrified miners gingerly opened the door and peered outside. All was quiet. They packed up and left quickly. As they set off down the trail the men saw one of the creatures emerge from the trees just 73 m (80 yards) away. Beck whipped out his rifle and fired. This time he did not miss. The creature collapsed. Falling over the edge of a canyon, it dropped 122 m (400 ft) to the rocks below.

When they got to Spirit Lake, the men reported their experience to the local rangers. The story soon got out, and a team of armed reporters hurried up into the hills sleeping bag and carried. He felt that they were going up and down hills, and at one point he was dragged along the ground. He could hear chattering and grunting.

Captured by Ape-Men

Cautiously he poked his head out of the sleeping bag. At first he could see little, but as the dawn came up he could gradually distinguish four huge figures. Ostman later described them as massively muscled, hairy apelike men. Recovering from his shock, Ostman reasoned that the creature who had brought him here must have had plenty of opportunity to kill him if it had wanted to do so. He looked around and saw that they were in a small area surrounded by sheer rocks, which had only one visible opening. The older male sat there as if keeping watch. After being left alone, Ostman set out to explore the area. He found a source of water and set up camp, all the time watching for an opportunity to escape. He considered shooting his way out, but he only had six bullets and did not think that this would be enough to kill four such massive animals.

Studying the Creatures

Ostman later claimed that he camped out with his kidnappers for several days, which gave him plenty of time to study them and their actions. The two larger creatures were over 2.13 m (7 ft) tall. Their heads were flat-faced, like those of humans, but were small in relation to their bodies, and they had no noticeable neck. They had low foreheads

TALE OF THE PARANORMAL

MUCHALAT HARRY

Four years after Ostman's encounter, another man claimed to be the victim of a similar kind of kidnapping. Muchalat Harry was a fur trapper from Vancouver Island who said he was taken from his camp one night and found himself captured by around twenty Sasquatch. Seeing a pile of gnawed bones nearby, he became terrified that he would be eaten. He managed to escape to tell his tale.

that sloped up to a peak at the rear, although some of this was made up of stiff hair. Their teeth were big and strong, and, although the older male had enlarged incisors, they were not big enough to be called tusks. According to Ostman, the creatures were active both by day and by night. They slept on what he described as blankets—sheets of woven bark and moss.

BIGFOOT: HITTING THE HEADLINES

The modern Bigfoot legend began in 1958, sparked by events at Bluff Creek in northern California. A road was being built through the area to aid the logging industry by opening the region up to heavy machinery. Ray Wallace was the head of the firm hired to do the job. His brother Wilbur was one of the foremen in charge of the task of clearing a flat roadbed through the rugged and densely forested terrain.

Nocturnal Intruder

On August 3, 1958, the workmen on the Bluff Creek road turned up for work to find some of their equipment disturbed. On August 27, the workmen discovered that the site had again been visited by something overnight, and this time it had left footprints. They were described as being exactly like those of a naked human foot, but much larger. At first Jerry Crew thought that someone was playing a practical joke, but after following the tracks and studying them more closely, he became convinced that they had really been left by a huge man of some kind. He went to see his foreman, Wilbur Wallace, who looked at the tracks. After some discussion, it was decided to ignore the strange nocturnal intruder—as long as he did not turn up in daylight hours when the work crew were on site.

On September 21, the local newspaper, the Humboldt Times, printed a letter from Mrs. Jesse Bemis, the wife of one of the workmen on the site, about the events up at Bluff Creek. Reporter Betty Allen then made the link between the mysterious giant footprints and the stories that had been circulating for years about a hairy man-ape that the local settlers and farmers called "Big Foot." Allen went out to talk to people who had actually seen the tracks of the man-ape. On September 28, she had a piece published about the creature she called "Bigfoot," which summed up the evidence to date.

Plaster Cast

On October 1, the Bluff Creek work gang found more footprints that had been left overnight. Wilbur Wallace asked his brother and boss, Ray Wallace, to come up to Bluff Creek to go over the situation. On October 3, they made a plaster cast of the clearest of the footprints. Crew took the cast down to the offices of the Humboldt Times. He and the cast were photographed and the photo was used to illustrate an article by the newspaper's editor Andrew Genzoli. The story was taken up and reprinted across the US and Canada, and then the rest of the world. A legend was born.

Back at Bluff Creek, the excitement mounted when, on October 12, two workers—Ray Kerr and Bob Breazle—claimed they actually saw the mysterious footprint-maker. According to them, they were driving along a local dirt road after dark when they momentarily caught a gigantic upright figure in their headlights. The creature ran off into the woods. The men described it as a hairy human figure well over 1.83 m (6 ft) tall. Newspaper reports of the events around Bluff Creek attracted two Yeti investigators, John Green and René Dahinden. Meanwhile, a friend of Crew's named Bob Titmus was out in the forests looking for signs of the mysterious creature. So far as is known, he was the first man ever to go looking for Sasquatch. He found some more footprints and took casts. Titmus, Green, and Dahinden would all devote huge amounts of time and effort to the search for the mystery creature. Between them they amassed a vast number of footprint casts, eyewitness accounts, hair samples, and other evidence.

A character destined to play a more controversial role in the story was Ray Wallace, the head of the road construction company. Wallace later admitted owning a pair of gigantic wooden feet with which he went about faking Bigfoot tracks.

Jerry Crew found enormous footprints in the soft mud at Bluff Creek.

APE-MAN FILE

DID RAY WALLACE FAKE ALL THE BLUFF CREEK FOOTPRINTS?

Skeptics believe that practical joker Wallace was responsible for all the footprints found at Bluff Creek, including the original ones found by Jerry Crew. They allege that Wallace's company was falling behind with its work and Wallace needed a reason to extend the deadline. On the other hand, Wallace was away from the state on business when at least some of the tracks appeared. Believers in the Sasquatch are more inclined to the view that Wallace took to his hoaxing as a result of events in Bluff Creek, which he then set out to exploit.

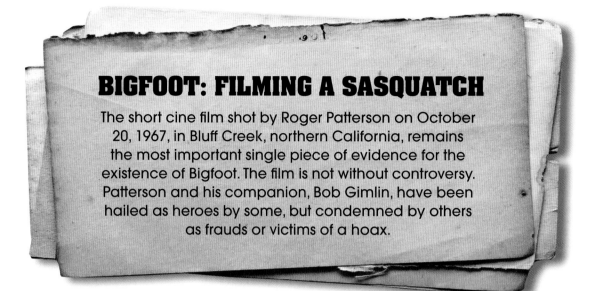

BIGFOOT: FILMING A SASQUATCH

The short cine film shot by Roger Patterson on October 20, 1967, in Bluff Creek, northern California, remains the most important single piece of evidence for the existence of Bigfoot. The film is not without controversy. Patterson and his companion, Bob Gimlin, have been hailed as heroes by some, but condemned by others as frauds or victims of a hoax.

The Tip-Off

In early October 1967, Patterson got a call. A Sasquatch investigator called Al Hodgson told Patterson that some excellent new tracks had been found in the Blue Creek Mountain area. It was thought that one set of very large footprints had been made by a big male, a smaller set of footprints by a female, and a third, much smaller set of prints by a juvenile. Patterson contacted his friend, Bob Gimlin. The pair arrived in the area on October 6, by which time heavy rains had washed away the tracks that Patterson had hoped to film. They agreed to stay, though, having come prepared for a two-week visit.

Encounter in a Canyon

On October 20, they decided to explore a rugged and remote canyon. They had been riding for hours when they reached a pile of fallen trees. The obstruction blocked their view up the canyon. According to the two men, as they came around the log jam they saw a Sasquatch beside the creek, about 24.5 m (80 ft) from them. The creature saw them at the same time, and it stood up abruptly and stared at them.

Patterson grabbed his movie-camera and moved toward the Sasquatch, which began to walk off along the creek bank. Patterson followed with the camera to his eye, trying to keep the Sasquatch in shot. He did not see a rise in the ground, so he tripped and fell. The Sasquatch turned to stare at him. Gimlin arrived and aimed his rifle at the creature, now only about 18 m (60 ft) away. The creature turned to look at them both, but did not break its stride. It continued to walk away and then passed around a bend in the canyon. That was when Patterson ran out of film, but the two men later said they could still hear the creature heading off. It seemed to be running quite fast.

Gimlin and Patterson hurriedly discussed the situation. Gimlin thought the creature had been nearly 213 cm (7 ft) tall and had weighed around 136 kg (300 lb). Patterson thought it had been 30 cm (1 ft) taller and much heavier.

The Footprints

By this time, it was late afternoon and the weather did not look too promising. Patterson wanted to go back to film and cast the footprints before night closed in. With a new film in the camera, he took extensive shots of the Sasquatch tracks and then cast the clearest footprints that he could find.

Patterson and Gimlin rode back to their camp, then drove to the town of Eureka to send out the precious movie film for processing. On the way back to camp they stopped off at Willow Creek to see Al Hodgson and told him about the day's events. Hodgson later recalled that Patterson was highly excited and was worrying about how good the film would prove to be.

Studying the Tracks

Word spread quickly among Sasquatch researchers, including Bob Titmus. Titmus decided to study the tracks for himself. He took some casts of the prints that Patterson had covered over with bark and twigs. According to Titmus, they showed the Sasquatch moving exactly as Patterson and Gimlin had claimed. Starting from the creek, the creature had gone upstream and then around the canyon corner, before disappearing into the trees.

APE-MAN FILE

OTHER FOOTAGE

Since 1967, other footage has surfaced claiming to show the Sasquatch, though none of it matches the quality of the Patterson film. These include the Freeman footage, shot in 1994 by forestry worker Paul Freeman near Walla Walla, Washington. It shows a hairy, humanlike figure crossing a path and then disappearing into woodland. The Redwoods footage (1995), filmed on a rainy night in northern California, shows a similar-looking creature moving in the beam of a car's headlights. The Manitoba footage (2005), shot on the banks of Nelson River, Manitoba, shows a strange figure on the opposite bank—but it is too distant to be sure what it is.

107

THE SKUNK APE

Reports of a mysterious wild ape from the southeastern United States have attracted much less publicity than the Bigfoot phenomenon of the northwestern states. Sasquatch researchers are divided in their reactions. Some treat the reports of the southeastern ape as if it were part of the same Sasquatch enigma. Others tend to ignore them because they do not fit the pattern for the Sasquatch of the forested mountains of the Pacific northwest. Still others, however, see them as evidence of something different from the Sasquatch. The southeastern creature has been called the Skunk Ape because of the terrible smell that is so often associated with its alleged appearances. The majority of the reports have come from Florida, so the creature is also sometimes called the Florida Ape.

Early Reports

The earliest reported sighting came in 1900. The local newspaper in Hannibal, Missouri, reported that a strange ape creature had been seen on an island in the Mississippi. It had been captured by a passing circus, which claimed that it was their escaped orangutan. They had not, however, reported a missing animal, and orangutans cannot swim, so its appearance on the island is something of a puzzle. A second report comes from 1949. Two fishermen out on Sugar Creek, Indiana, were allegedly chased off by a rather aggressive creature that they identified as a "gorilla." However, it was not until the 1960s that reports began to be made in any real numbers.

One of the first of these came from Davis, West Virginia, in 1960. A group of young men were camping out in some woods. One of them felt a sudden dig in his ribs. Thinking it was a friend wanting his attention, he turned around. Instead, according to the witness, he found himself looking at an 244-cm (8-ft) tall figure covered in long, shaggy hair. The creature had enormous eyes that glowed. After frightening the teenager, the beast allegedly walked off into the trees.

Another reported sighting came from Clanton, Alabama, in the same year. The Reverend E.C. Hand and half a dozen others claimed they saw an ape bounding along beside Route 31. They called Sheriff T.J. Lockhart, who went to investigate. He found two sets of tracks, one larger than the other.

Glowing Eyes

On the evening of November 30, 1966, a woman got a puncture while driving

along a rural road near Brooksville, Florida. She got out to change the wheel and was halfway through the process when she saw something moving in the trees. According to her later testimony, she saw an apelike figure covered in hair. As it got closer, she said, the figure's eyes seemed to glow a weird green as they reflected the light from her flashlight. She got back into her car and waited for a passing vehicle that she could flag down.

Seen from a Car

Many reported sightings of Skunk Apes have been by motorists in rural areas. For instance, a woman was driving back to her rural home in December 1985 after completing her night shift at work. Driving along the highway from Tavares, she allegedly saw a large animal move out of the woods. The creature, she later said, was walking on its hind legs, but she did not get a good look. She slowed down as she passed the place where it had entered

the trees and rolled down the car window. Although she could not see anything, she said she was hit by a deeply offensive stench.

APE-MAN FILE

SIMIAN SIMILARITIES

Based on the reports of sightings, the Skunk Ape would seem to be quite a different creature from the Sasquatch of the Pacific northwest. The Sasquatch is routinely described as being a massive creature walking upright like a human. In comparison, the Skunk Ape is usually reported as being smaller, and it either walks on all fours or with a waddling gait if upright. It is generally described as being very like a chimpanzee or an orangutan.

Too Close for Comfort

The Sasquatch of the northwestern United States is typically described as a placid, shy creature that would sooner avoid encounters with humans. Occasionally though, reports come in of a creature that—possibly driven by hunger—ventures into human homes. These have mostly come from the eastern US. Among the more famous of these reports was a string of cases from around Fouke in Kentucky. They told of a Bigfoot-type creature that behaved in a hostile way toward humans. Typical of these was the Ford case.

On the night of May 1, 1971, Mrs. Ford was woken up by the sound of her bedroom window opening. Through the open window, so she later claimed, came a hairy arm bearing a large, clawed hand that grasped out for her. Behind the window, Mrs. Ford said she glimpsed an apelike face. When she screamed, the arm and the face retreated. Mr. Ford grabbed a gun and ran out of the house. He said he arrived just in time to see a Sasquatch figure. He fired, but

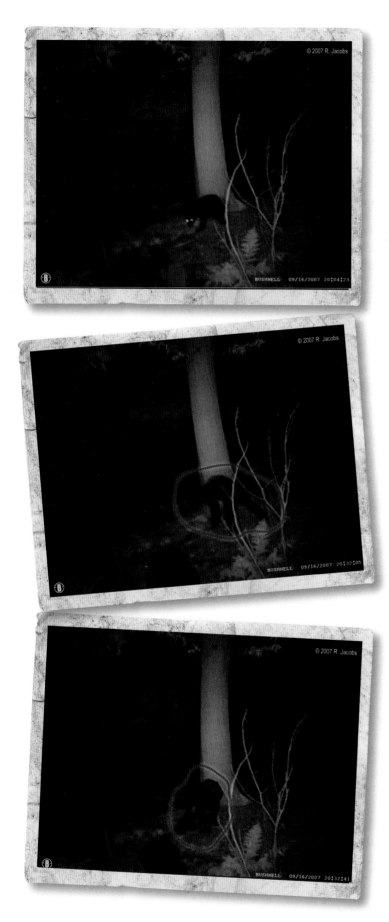

The so-called Jacobs photos were taken in Pennsylvania in 2007 by a camera set up to record a family of bears. Is the skinny, ape-like creature a Sasquatch?

the creature apparently slipped off into the trees unharmed. An hour later, the couple reported, the beast came back, on this occasion trying to kick the front door down. Ford shot at it again, and this time it left for good.

Disrupted Picnic

Joan Mills and Mary Ryan stopped for a picnic near the town of Louisiana, Missouri, in July 1971. They had just laid out their meal when—so they later reported—a Bigfoot came lumbering out of some nearby bushes. It was making what they described as a weird gurgling noise and was behaving in a threatening manner. The two women fled to their car and locked themselves in, but they could not drive away because they had left the keys with their picnic. Then, according to their report, the Bigfoot lumbered up to the car and tried to open the doors. Unable to do so, it turned to the picnic and ate some food before returning to the undergrowth from which it had emerged. Once it was gone, Mills retrieved the keys, and they drove off.

In the same month, a Bigfoot allegedly visited a farm near Shapsville, Indiana, on five separate occasions. Each time, according to the farmer, it came at night, and once it attacked the farm dog, though without inflicting serious injury. The farmer said he shot at it several times, but never seemed able to hit the thing.

A couple of years later, in June 1973, four teenage girls were in a car sheltering from a thunderstorm when they were allegedly

approached by a 244-cm (8-ft) tall Bigfoot that growled and screamed at them. The beast, they said, had large eyes that glowed bright red. Although the teenagers drove off at high speed, the Bigfoot seemed able to move even quicker because they apparently saw it standing beside the road ahead of them as they sped off. When they reached the home of one of the girls, the Bigfoot was waiting—so they say. After glaring at them with its red eyes, it walked off.

THE YETI

The Yeti—or "Abominable Snowman," as the press called it—hit the news headlines in the year 1951. British mountaineer Eric Shipton returned from an expedition to the Himalayas with some photographs taken in the high mountain snows. They were of a series of footprints that ran for hundreds of yards across a snowfield. Although the footprints were roughly human in outline, they were enormous. The photographs dominated the British newspapers for days and the story rapidly spread to other countries.

The purpose of Shipton's Himalayan trip had been to discover routes up the lower sections of the Everest massif in readiness for a later attempt on the peak itself. Shipton and his colleague Michael Ward were exploring the saddle at the top of the Menlung Glacier at around 5,486 m (18,000 ft) when they saw a set of tracks left in deep snow. They followed them for about 1,600 m (1 mile) along the edge of the glacier, but then had to turn back. In order to prove their story, they photographed a section of the track and one of the clearest individual prints.

Early Encounters

Even if the general public was surprised by these pictures, mountaineers and hikers in the Himalayas were less shocked. For decades, they had been hearing stories about the strange half-human, half-ape beasts that lurked in the mountains. The only surprise was that somebody had finally managed to photograph a series of tracks.

This photograph sparked international interest in the Yeti.

The first outsider to hear tales of the strange beasts was the hill walker B.H. Hodgson. He was in northern Nepal in 1825 when his porters reported seeing a tall creature covered with long, dark hair, which bounded off in apparent fear. Hodgson did not see the creature himself, but, from the descriptions given by his excited porters, he thought that it must have been some sort of orangutan.

In 1889, Major L.A. Waddell was on a mapping expedition in the mountains of Sikkim when he found a trackway of footprints that seemed to be those of a barefooted man with enormous feet. His guide declared that they belonged to "the hairy wild man" and insisted that they should leave the area at once.

In 1925, Narik Tombazi, a Fellow of the Royal Geographical Society, reported an encounter with the Abominable Snowman. He was studying glaciers in northern Sikkim when he claims he saw a strange figure moving slowly along a path about 610 m (2,000 ft) below him. The creature was walking upright like a human, but it was covered in dense fur. It stopped every now and then to pluck leaves from bushes and once to uproot a bush and gnaw on its roots.

TALE OF THE PARANORMAL

A WARNING CRY

In 1899, Mary MacDonald, the daughter of a colonial officer, was walking through the Himalayan mountains. She was on a month-long hiking trip and had a team of porters to carry her tent, cooking equipment, and supplies. As the column was about to enter a narrow gorge on the way to the Garbyang Pass, the rocks echoed to a strange call. MacDonald later likened it to the call of a seagull, but very much louder, ending in a throaty roar. Puzzled, MacDonald turned around to ask her guide what animal could make such a noise. She found herself alone. Her guide and porters had thrown down their loads and were running away at high speed back down the track.

Now rather worried, MacDonald retrieved her hunting rifle from one of the abandoned packs, in case the unknown animal turned out to be dangerous, and set off after her porters. She found them grouped on a flat area of ground some 3.2 km (2 miles) from the gorge. They told her that the cry had been made by a *metoh kangmi*, or "bad man of the snow," which was warning them to leave. It was only after much persuasion and some threats that MacDonald got her men to retrieve the abandoned packs, but nothing would persuade them to enter the gorge.

Figures on a Mountainside

In September 1921, Colonel Howard-Bury was near Lhapka-la on his way to scout out Mount Everest for a climbing expedition. Suddenly his porters started chattering excitedly to each other and then began pointing to the side of a mountain 800 m (half a mile) or so ahead. Howard-Bury looked for the source of their interest and saw—so he later alleged—three humanlike figures walking across a large patch of snow. Some hours later the expedition reached the snowfield, and he was able to study the tracks left by the figures. Each footprint, he later reported, was over 40 cm (14 in) long, but otherwise looked like that of a naked human foot. The porters told Howard-Bury that the figures were not men but *metoh kangmi*.

APE-MAN FILE

WHAT'S IN A NAME?

Colonel Howard-Bury translated the phrase *metoh kangmi* as "Abominable Snowman." He passed on the story to a Calcutta-based journalist named Henry Newman, who wrote a few pieces about the mystery animal, again calling it the Abominable Snowman. This was the name that was used when tales of the mystery creature first spread through the English-speaking communities of northern India.

In the postwar period the name "Yeti" began to be applied to the creature. The word is not, in fact, very accurate, being derived from *yeh-the*, a generic Nepalese term for any large animal that lives in the high mountains. This has led to some confusion over the years. Locals may refer to the Himalayan red bear as a *yeh-the*, since it is large and lives in the high mountains. Many later visitors who heard stories about the aggressive Yeti had in fact been listening to tales of encounters with the red bear.

The 1954 Expedition

In 1954, the British *Daily Mail* financed an expedition to the Himalayas. The aim was to collect information about the Yeti—and catch one, if possible. The expedition leaders hired 300 porters to carry the equipment up into the high mountains, where hundreds of locals were contacted and vast distances were covered. No Yeti was captured, nor even seen, but the expedition did come back with a wealth of anecdotal evidence and a great boost in sales for the newspaper.

Among the more exciting discoveries of the expedition was the fact that two Yeti scalps were allegedly kept in Buddhist monasteries at Pangboche and Khumjung. They were used in temple rituals and dances by monks who pretended to be Yetis. The *Daily Mail* team was allowed to photograph the Pangboche scalp, but they could not borrow it for study. In 1960, the mountaineer Sir Edmund Hillary was allowed to borrow the Khumjung scalp in return for having the

This scalp and hand, alleged to have belonged to a Yeti, were kept for many years at the remote Pangboche Monastery.

monastic school rebuilt. Tests revealed that the skin had come from the hide of a serow, a form of wild Himalayan goat.

Could the Yeti Be an Ape?

Many Yeti seekers hold fast to the belief that the creature is some unclassified species of ape. They speculate that a small population of a species previously thought extinct might have survived in the remote forests of the Himalayas. The fossil record for apes, particularly those in Asia, is sparse, but the few remains that have turned up show that apes were once far more widely distributed across southern Asia than they are today.

One of these was the massive *Gigantopithecus*, which apparently became extinct around 150,000 years ago. This ape lived across India, Southeast Asia, and southern China.

Fossils of the ape reveal it was a massive 2.73 m (9 ft) tall on its hind legs. Could the Yeti, if it exists, be descended from *Gigantopithecus* or some other ape species long thought dead? We simply don't know.

THE MARICOXI

In recent years the word "Maricoxi" has become a generic term for any of the cryptid primates that are said to live in the tropical rainforests of South America. These go by such names as Aluxes, Goazis, Aigypans, Vasitris, Matuyus, Curupiras, Curinqueans, Didi, Mono Grande, and Mapinguary. Whether or not each name indicates a different cryptid is unclear. Some or all of the names might refer to the same creature.

Hairy Hominids

The Maricoxi themselves are, or were, supposedly an extremely primitive tribe of hominids living in the Mato Grosso, a vast upland region of southern Brazil and northern Paraguay made up of forest and dense scrub. The Maricoxi were allegedly discovered by the English explorer Percy Fawcett in 1914. According to his description of the encounter with the ferocious tribe, he barely escaped with his life. He described the Maricoxi as apelike people, completely covered in hair, who spoke in grunts. Yet they lived in villages and used bows and arrows.

The Mono Grande and the Didi

Another cryptid ape-man of South America is the Mono Grande, which translates as "giant monkey." This hair-covered beast is usually described as standing about 1.5 m (6 ft) tall. It allegedly reacts badly to

According to Bigfoot believers, the rainforests of South America could be home to several different species of ape-men.

MAN OF THE WOODS

The first outsider to record stories of hair-covered humans was the German naturalist Alexander von Humboldt, who mapped much of the Orinoco River in the early 1800s. He wrote:

"On the Orinoco, people speak of the existence of a hairy man of the woods called Salvaje, that carries off women, constructs huts, and sometimes eats human flesh. The Tamanacs call him Achi, and the Maypures named him Vasitri or 'great devil.' The natives and the missionaries have no doubt of the existence of this man-shaped monkey, of which they entertain a singular dread. Father Gili (a local missionary) gravely relates the history of a lady in the town of San Carlos, in the Llanos of Venezuela, who much praised the gentle character and attentions of the man of the woods. She is stated to have lived several years with one in great domestic harmony, and only requested some hunters to take her back, 'because she and her children (a little hairy also) were weary of living far from the church and the sacraments.'"

humans, thrashing branches, screaming aggressively, and charging at intruders. These seem to be mere displays, however, because very few people have reported being injured by a Mono Grande.

Another legendary creature goes by the name of the Didi. The creature is very similar to the Mono Grande. Both live in the dense rainforests of northern South America. They are also about the same size and have similar habits. The only difference seems to be that the Mono Grande has a short tail, while the Didi has none. The naturalist Edward Bancroft wrote in his *An Essay on the Natural History of Guiana* (1769): "It is much larger than either the African ape (chimpanzee) or the Oriental ape (orangutan), if the accounts of the natives may be relied upon. They are represented by the Indians as being near 1.5 m (5 ft) in height, maintaining an erect position, and having a human form, thinly covered with short black hair, but I suspect that their height has been augmented by the fears of the Indians who greatly dread them."

Melancholy Whistle

In 1868, the explorer Charles Barrington Brown was on the Upper Mazaruni when he heard a most peculiar animal call. He described it as "... a long, loud, and most melancholy whistle. Two or three times the whistle was repeated, beginning in a high key and dying gradually away into a low one." Brown asked his local porters what had made the cry. They told him that it was the Didi, which they described as "a short, thickset, and powerful wild man whose body is covered with hair and who lives in the forest." Brown later met a man who had stumbled across a male and female Didi when out chopping timber one day. They had attacked him, scratching him badly, but he had defended himself and they had fled.

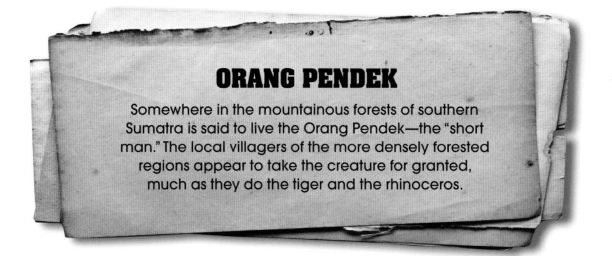

ORANG PENDEK

Somewhere in the mountainous forests of southern Sumatra is said to live the Orang Pendek—the "short man." The local villagers of the more densely forested regions appear to take the creature for granted, much as they do the tiger and the rhinoceros.

Reports from Europeans

The first reference to this creature to be written by an outsider was made in 1917 by a Dr. Edward Jacobson. He said that he had been camped near Boekit Kaba when the local men he had hired to hunt meat for him came strolling in to announce that they had just passed an Orang Pendek. It had been looking for insect larvae in a fallen

NERVOUS ENCOUNTER

In 1923, a Dutch explorer named Van Herwaarden was out hunting wild pigs on the island of Poeloe Rimau, off Sumatra, when he saw something unusual sitting in a tree:

"I discovered a dark and hairy creature on a branch. The front of its body was pressed tightly against the tree. It looked as if it were trying to make itself inconspicuous and felt that it was about to be discovered. I laid my gun on the ground and tried to get nearer the animal…. The creature lifted itself a little from the branch and leaned over the side so that I could then see its hair, its forehead, and a pair of eyes which stared at me. Its movements had at first been slow and cautious, but, as soon as the thing saw me, the whole situation changed. It became nervous and trembled all over…. There was nothing repulsive or ugly about the face, nor was it at all ape-like, although the quick nervous movements of its eyes and mouth were very like those of a monkey in distress. I began to talk in a calm and friendly way as if I were soothing a frightened dog or horse, but it did not make much difference. When I raised my gun, I heard a plaintive 'hu-hu,' which was at once answered by similar calls from the forest nearby. I laid my gun on the ground and climbed into the tree again. The beast ran very fast along a branch, then dropped 3 m (10 ft) to the ground. By the time I reached my gun, it was 27 m (30 yards) away and running fast, giving a sort of whistle. Many people may think me childish if I say that, when I saw its flying hair in the sights, I did not pull the trigger. I suddenly felt that I was going to commit murder."

log. They said that the creature had run off when it had seen them. After further questioning, Jacobson learned that the creature had run off on its hind legs. Jacobson thought this odd because the only apes he knew of, gibbons and orangutans, would have swung off through the trees. He went to investigate and allegedly found a footprint that looked exactly like that of a human, except that it was very small.

Jacobson's report prompted a separate account from another European living in Sumatra, L.C. Westenenk. He stated that a friend of his had been leading a gang of workmen into the forest near Loeboek Salasik to cut timber when they came across what he described as: "... a large creature, low on its feet, which ran like a man and was about to cross the path. It was very hairy and was not an orangutan. Its face was not like an ordinary man's. It silently and gravely gave the men a disagreeable stare and ran calmly away. The workmen ran faster in the opposite direction."

ASIAN WILD MEN

There have been hundreds of reports coming out of Central Asia about a creature that is neither fully human nor entirely animal. It goes by many names, including Abnuaaya, Barmanu, Bekk-Bok, Biabin-Guli, Gul-Biavan, Guli-Avan, Golub-Yavan, Kaptar, Kra-Dhan, Ksy Gyik, Mirygdy, Mulen, and Voita. However, researchers have needed a general term when referring to these creatures. Those studying reports from China tend to call the beast the Yeren, while those looking at reports from Mongolia and the former Soviet Union call it Almas, or sometimes Almasti.

What Is It and Where Does It Live?

Theories abound about what the legendary creature might be. Some researchers speculate that, if it exists, it may be an unknown primate. Others argue that it may be a bear or a monkey, and still others suggest it could be a creature halfway between ape and human.

Ivlov's Encounter

One of the first outsiders to take an interest in the Almas-Yeren was a Russian doctor by the name of Ivan Ivlov. In the autumn of 1963, he was exploring the Altai Mountains when he spotted three figures some distance away on a mountain slope. Ivlov took out his binoculars to get a better view. He later reported that the shape of the figures, and the way they moved, was human but that they were covered in hair. There was a male, a slightly smaller female, and a child. The creatures seemed to be digging, perhaps for roots to eat. When they saw Ivlov, they moved off. They rounded a rock crag and disappeared from sight. Ivlov was puzzled and turned to his Mongolian companions. They told him that the figures were wild men. They explained that the wild men were not really humans, but were more like animals.

Ivlov was intrigued, and, throughout the rest of his journey, he quizzed his companions about these mysterious wild men. He learned that the local herdsmen did not think that the humanlike creatures were at all mysterious or unusual: they were just another part of the local wildlife. One local told Ivlov of the time an Almas male had scooped up a juvenile when it spotted the Mongolian approaching. As the adult Almas strode off, the youngster peered over its shoulder at the human, then stuck its tongue out and made faces—a remarkably human response.

Used for Medicine

Published in the Qing Dynasty in around the year 1664 was a book entitled *The Mirror of Medicine*. It was a compendium of wild animals to be found in northern China and Mongolia and suggested ways their parts could be used for treating illnesses. Among the assorted wildlife, it included this entry: "The wild man lives in the northern mountains, and his origins are like that of the bear. His body resembles that of a man, and he has enormous strength. His meat may be eaten to treat mental disease. His gall cures jaundice." Alongside the text was a small illustration. It showed a basically human figure standing on a rock with its left arm upraised. The entire body of the creature,

The Almas has—according to witnesses—been known to wear rudimentary clothing.

except for its feet and hands, was covered in dense fur. Even the eyes and the mouth were surrounded by hair.

THE AUSTRALIAN YOWIE

For many decades, the wooded hills of eastern Australia have yielded reports of a creature that is sometimes called the Hairy Fellah but is more commonly termed the Yowie. The latter name grew out of one of the many Aboriginal terms for this creature in New South Wales (NSW). Other terms for the creature, from the various Aboriginal languages, include gulaga, thoolalgarl, doolagarl, myngawin, and joogabinna.

Aboriginal Stories

Traditional Aboriginal stories about this creature often feature elements of the supernatural. For instance, the Dulugars of the Suggan Buggan can allegedly fly through the air, and the Quinkin of the Yalanji people is apparently a demon taller than a tree. The Yaroma, meanwhile, are said to have mouths so large that they can swallow men whole.

EYEWITNESS ACCOUNT

UNEARTHLY LOOKING BEING

In 1876, no fewer than nine Europeans were on the Laachlan River when they saw, according to one of them: "... an inhuman, unearthly looking being, bearing in every way the shape of a man, with a big red face, hands, and legs covered with long shaggy hair. The head was covered with dark, grissly hair, the face with shaggy, dark hair, the back and belly with hair of a lighter shade. This devil-devil, or whatever it may be called, doubled round and fled."

As European settlers began overrunning Aboriginal lands, they began to hear reports of Yowies. Black Harry, a leader of the Ngunnawal people, reported that in about 1847 he had seen a group of warriors attack and kill one of these creatures on the banks of the Murrumbidgee River. He said that the mystery creature was "like a black man, but covered all over with white hair."

European Reports

A number of Europeans began to claim sightings of the hairy creatures, too. In 1882, H.J. McCooey came across a creature near Batemans Bay, NSW. "My attention was attracted by the cries of a number of birds, which were pursuing and darting at it. It was partly upright, looking up at the birds, blinking its eyes, and making a chattering sound. The creature was nearly 1.50 m (5 ft) tall and covered with very long black hair which was dirty red about the throat and breast. Its eyes, which were small and restless, were partly hidden by matted hair. The length of the arms seemed out of proportion. It would probably have weighed about 51 kg (112 lbs)." McCooey threw a stone at it, and the creature ran off.

In 1912, Charles Harper was camping out on Currickbilly Ridge, NSW, with two companions when they heard a "low rumbling growl" coming from the darkness. One of the men threw a handful of twigs onto the embers of the camp fire, causing flames to spring up and illuminate the creature that had been making the noise. Harper later recorded it as being "a huge man-like animal growling, grimacing, and thumping his breast with his huge, hand-like paws. I should say its height would be 173–179 cm (5 ft 8 in–5 ft 10 in). Its body, legs, and arms were covered with long, brownish-red hair, which shook with every quivering movement of its body.

"The hair on its shoulders and back parts appeared in the light of the fire to be jet black and long; but what struck me as most extraordinary was the apparently human shape, but still so very different. The body frame was enormous, indicating immense strength and power of endurance. The arms and forepaws were long and large, and very muscular, being covered with shorter hair. The head and face were small but very human. The eyes were large, dark, and piercing, deeply set. A most horrible mouth was ornamented with two large and long canine tooth. When the jaws were closed, they protruded over the lower lip." Harper added that the creature stood watching the men for a few seconds, then dropped onto all fours and raced off into the bush.

Reports indicate that the Yowie is rather more human than some of its fellow cryptid humanoids.

GLOSSARY

archaeologist A scholar of human history and prehistory through the excavation of sites and analysis of artifacts and other physical remains.

artifact An object made by a human being, typically something of cultural or historical interest.

asteroid A small rocky body orbiting the Sun. A few enter the Earth's atmosphere as meteors.

autopsy A postmortem examination to discover the cause of death.

bilocation The phenomenon of appearing in two places at once.

Buddhism An Asian religion or philosophy founded by Siddartha Gautama in north-eastern India in the 5th century BCE.

"buzz" (slang) Fly very close to (another aircraft, the ground, etc.) at a high speed.

cast A three-dimensional shape, such as a footprint, made by shaping a material (such as plaster of Paris).

cataclysm A large-scale violent event in the natural world.

channelling Serving as a medium for a spirit.

clairvoyant Having the supernatural ability to perceive events in the future.

comet A celestial object consisting of a nucleus of ice and dust and, when near the Sun, a "tail" of gas and dust particles.

conquistadors The Spanish conquerors of Mexico and Peru in the 16th century.

cryptid A creature that appears in stories and legends, but whose existence is not acknowledged by science.

cryptozoologist A person who studies cryptids.

deluge A flood.

discarnate (of a person or being) Not having a physical body.

doppelgänger An apparition or double of a living person.

extraterrestrial Relating to something from outside the Earth or its atmosphere.

generic Relating to a class or group of things; not specific.

geologist A scientist who studies the Earth's physical structure and substance, its history, and the processes that act on it.

hallucination An experience involving the apparent perception of something not present.

hominid A primate of the family Hominidae that includes humans and their extinct ancestors.

humanoid Having an appearance resembling that of a human.

hypnosis The induction of a state of consciousness in which a person apparently loses the power of voluntary action and is highly responsive to suggestion or direction.

hypnotic regression A process of taking a person back to an earlier stage of life through hypnosis.

incapacitate Prevent from functioning in a normal way.

medium A person claiming to be in contact with the spirits of the dead and able to communicate between the dead and the living.

meteorite A meteor that survives its passage through the Earth's atmosphere and strikes the ground.

meteors Small bodies of matter from outer space that enter the Earth's atmosphere and appear as streaks of light.

mirage An optical illusion caused by atmospheric conditions.

near-death experience An experience taking place on the brink of death and recounted by a person after recovery, typically an out-of-body experience or a vision of a tunnel of light.

occultist A follower of supernatural, mystical, or magical beliefs and practices.

paranormal Describing events or phenomena that are beyond the scope of normal scientific understanding.

petroglyph A rock carving, especially an ancient one.

phenomena (plural of phenomenon) Facts or situations that are observed to exist or happen.

plaster (of Paris) A soft white substance made by the addition of water to powdered gypsum, which hardens when dried. It is used for making sculptures and casts.

poltergeist A ghost or other supernatural being supposedly responsible for physical disturbances such as loud noises and objects thrown around.

possession The state of being controlled by a demon or spirit.

precognition Foreknowledge of an event, especially of a paranormal kind.

premonition A strong feeling that something is about to happen, especially something unpleasant.

primate A mammal of an order that includes monkeys, apes, and humans. They are distinguished by having hands, handlike feet, and forward-facing eyes.

pseudoscientific Beliefs or practices mistakenly regarded as being based on scientific method.

psychic A person considered or claiming to have psychic powers; a medium.

reincarnation The rebirth of a soul in a new body.

resuscitate To revive (someone) from unconsciousness or apparent death.

séance A meeting at which people attempt to make contact with the dead, especially with the help of a medium.

seismic Relating to earthquakes or other vibrations of the Earth and its crust.

telepathic communication The supposed communication of thoughts and ideas by means other than the known senses.

trance A half-conscious state characterized by an absence of response to external stimuli.

trauma A deeply distressing or disturbing experience.

USAF United States Air Force.

weather balloon A balloon equipped with special equipment that is sent into the atmosphere to provide information about the weather.

125

INDEX